Passion *and* Purity

"Passion and Purity couldn't
be more timely,
more on target"
—Ruth Bell Graham

"This book is definitely for men, too"
—Billy Graham

"Rainbows are made of sunlight and rain. The sunlight, which turned my world into a radiance of color, was the knowledge of Jim Elliot's love. The rain was the other fact he explained to me as we sat on the grass by the Lagoon—that God was calling him to remain single. Perhaps for life, perhaps only until he had firsthand experience in the place where he was to work as a jungle missionary. Older missionaries had told him that single men were needed to do jobs married ones could never do. There were some areas where women could not go. Jim took their word for it and committed himself to bachelorhood for as long as the will of God required."

Five years passed before Jim Elliot knew that it was God's will that he and Elisabeth marry. During those five years both experienced the same feelings that you may now have—loneliness . . . longing . . . impatience . . . hope . . . fear of what may lie ahead combined with trust in God . . . the elation of love mingled with the pain of separation. Through their time of waiting upon the Lord, both grew in faith and their love was purified. They learned many lessons which Elisabeth Elliot now shares with you. You, too, will learn to let your heart rest "where true joys are to be found."

Passion *and* Purity

Learning to Bring Your Love Life
Under Christ's Control

Elisabeth Elliot

Revell

a division of Baker Publishing Group
Grand Rapids, Michigan

© 1984, 2002 by Elisabeth Elliot

Published by Revell
a division of Baker Publishing Group
P.O. Box 6287, Grand Rapids, MI 49516-6287
www.revellbooks.com

Repackaged edition published 2013

Printed in the United States of America

ISBN 978-0-8007-2313-2

Library of Congress Cataloging-in-Publication Data is on file at the Library of Congress, Washington, D.C.

Unless otherwise indicated, Scripture is taken from the King James Version of the Bible.

Scripture marked PHILLIPS is taken from The New Testament In Modern English, revised edition—J. B. Phillips, translator. © J. B. Phillips 1958, 1960, 1972. Used by permission of Macmillan Publishing Co., Inc.

Scripture marked YOUNG CHURCHES is taken from LETTERS TO YOUNG CHURCHES by J. B. Phillips. Copyright © 1947, 1957 by Macmillan Publishing Co., Inc., renewed 1975 by J. B. Phillips. Used by permission.

Scripture marked NEB is taken from The New English Bible, Copyright © 1961, 1970, 1989, by The Delegates of Oxford University Press and The Syndics of the Cambridge University Press. Reprinted by permission.

Quotation from "The Shooting of Dan McGrew," by Robert Service, reprinted by permission of DODD, MEAD, & COMPANY, INC. from THE COLLECTED POEMS OF ROBERT SERVICE.

Quotation from TOWARD JERUSALEM copyrighted material used by permission of the Christian Literature Crusade, Fort Washington, PA 19034.

"Night Song at Amalfi" reprinted with permission of Macmillan Publishing Company from COLLECTED POEMS by Sara Teasdale. Copyright 1915 by Macmillan Publishing Co., Inc., renewed 1943 by Mamie T. Wheless.

15   16   17   18   19   7   6   5   4   3   2

Contents

Foreword

There's a path near my home that I enjoy taking walks on. It winds through woods and beside a pond dotted with Canada Geese. One day after strolling on it for nearly ten minutes I realized that I'd been absentmindedly staring down at my feet the entire time. When I looked up it seemed the world switched from black and white to color. The sky was a piercing blue, the autumn leaves on the trees towering above were bright orange, yellow, and red. Silly isn't it? That beauty surrounded me and instead of enjoying it I was looking down at my shoddy pair of tennis shoes on the black asphalt.

I share this story because I think it illustrates a tendency we have when it comes to the topic of romance and relationships. Too often we have a *downward* gaze—we lock our eyes on the drab tones of what we want, need, or deserve from a relationship. And sadly, there are countless books ready to feed this wrong perspective. They promise "self-empowerment" and offer endless advice for squeezing out every last drop of self-fulfillment from a relationship.

Fortunately for you and me, there are writers like Elisabeth Elliot. The book you're holding tells a very moving love story. It's honest. It's practical. But even as it addresses the real questions and concerns of single men and women it always lifts our gaze upward—above our immediate pre-occupations, above our longings for human companion-ship to the Maker who created us for Himself. There is so much wonder and beauty awaiting those who will view the path of relationships as a chance to gaze on the good-ness and creativity of God. This book will help you do that.

I hope that you'll read these pages differently than I first did. I was 16 and in the middle of a serious dating rela-tionship when my mom gave me a copy of *Passion & Purity*. I was immediately suspicious of the subtitle which read, "Learning to bring your love life under Christ's control." I was sure it was going to tell me that I wasn't allowed to kiss my girlfriend (something I thought very vital to my continued happiness at the time). So what did I do? I deter-mined before I had even cracked the cover that I was going to disagree with everything it had to say. As my mom now jokes, I read all the "passion" but skipped all the "purity." What a mistake!

A few years later I reread *Passion & Purity* and realized that its message was exactly what I needed to hear in the midst of my high-school dating relationship. Why had it seemed so irrelevant? Why didn't I learn from it at that time? Because I decided from the beginning that I wasn't going to listen.

Please don't make my mistake. Please read this book with humility. When you come to something you think you disagree with or to a standard of purity that seems too high, ask God to give you His perspective. Keep reading and ask Him to change your heart if you're in the wrong.

Read it prayerfully. It's not merely information or tech-niques for "catching" a spouse. It's full of truth and wis-dom. Like its author, it is steeped in God's word. Take your time as you read and when you sense God emphasizing something, pause to commune with him. Ask Him to bring appropriate conviction. Ask Him to deepen your faith and your love for Him.

God used this book to radically change my attitude toward romantic relationships. If you read it with humility and prayer, I believe it can do the same for you.

Five years ago, at age twenty-one, I typed with trembling hands a letter to Mrs. Elliot to ask if she'd be willing to look over the unpublished manuscript of a book I'd written called *I Kissed Dating Goodbye*. (Needless to say I'd come a long way from my views as a sixteen-year-old.) I rewrote that letter at least three times. In one discarded version I told Mrs. Elliot that I doubted my book was even worth publishing since hers was so much better. And because I endlessly quoted her I suggested that I "just forget my book and work at selling yours."

I'll never forget the day I received a post-card reply from her. She had read my book and said I'd done a good job, that I'd written a worthwhile book. I was elated. I still have that little note taped in my journal.

What an honor it is for me to return the favor and commend *Passion and Purity* to any single person seeking a biblical vision of romantic relationships. This book is a classic. It's written by one of my heroes.

Thank you, Mrs. Elliot, for sharing your love story—both your love for Mr. Elliot and your love for your Savior. Thanks for writing the truths of God's word to my generation. Because of your faithfulness many are gazing outward and upward at the beauty of our great God.

Joshua Harris

"The only place outside Heaven where you can be perfectly safe from all the dangers and perturbations of love is Hell."

C.S. Lewis
The Four Loves

Preface

In my day we would have called them love affairs or romances. Now they are called relationships. The word *love* has fallen on bad times. To many people it means nothing more nor less than going to bed with somebody, never mind what sex the other may belong to. Bumper stickers substitute a picture of a red heart for the word *love* and apply it to just about anything, anybody, or any place. In some Christian gatherings people are asked to turn around and look the person next to them full in the face, even if he is a perfect stranger, and say, with a broad smile and without the least trace of a blush, "God loves you, and so do I," and prove it by a hearty bear hug. This apparently makes some of them feel good. Perhaps it even convinces them they've obeyed the strongest and toughest command ever laid on human beings: Love one another *as Christ has loved you*. No wonder people cast about for some other word to describe what they feel for an individual of the opposite sex. It's new. It's neat. It's really neat. It's special.

"What's special?" I sometimes ask.

"Well, you know, this, like, relationship."

"What relationship, exactly?"

"Well, I don't know, you know, it's like, I mean, it's just really neat."

A schoolteacher wrote to me recently about a "growing friendship" with a man she had been riding to work with. He had gone to a distant state, and she was feeling very lonely and uncertain about the future. She was not sure just what their relationship had been or was now or might turn out to be, but having picked up from my writings bits and pieces that refer to matters of the heart, she wanted to know more.

"I want to know a little of what you were thinking, if I may. What were your feelings? What was going through your mind? Did your emotions often conflict with your thinking? If you can spare a few minutes and write back, I would hold on to any words of wisdom you have."

Of course I spared the few minutes. The letters keep coming, bombarding me with questions along these lines, suggesting that the experience of one from a different generation might still be a signpost. Here are snippets from other letters:

"I am writing to you as a young woman seeking as honestly as I know how to be obedient to God, to know wisdom and discernment, to be pleasing and faithful and to wait on Him. My walk with Christ is rather an alone one. I lack knowing the spiritual leadership of a woman who is older than I. I know that concerning some things it was intended that the older women instruct the younger. I know that you are a servant, and I hope that you might respond."

"How should a woman behave if a man is not fulfilling his role?"

"How shall I know that this woman is right for me?"

"How far can we go without a commitment to marriage? How far if we have that commitment?"

"What is our role as single women—waiting around?"

"You seem so strong and unswerving in your faith. Over and over I tell God I cannot go through this anymore. I quit. I tell Him I am mad. Don't you ever falter and feel you cannot go on? Have you never had times of giving up?"

"Did you struggle with the desire to be with Jim all the years you were separated?"

"Did you struggle with being single if your heart yearned for Jim?"

"If Tom had not come into my life, all my thoughts would be focused on the Lord. There would be no conflict. It bothers me so—I am lonely, and cry so easily, almost as if my heart is breaking. Is this part of God's plan?"

"*How* did you handle the impatience of wanting to be with the man you loved?"

I answer all the letters that come. I find myself trying to put into words, again and again, the lessons that came out of my own experience. I've been there where these men and women are. I know exactly what they mean. I fear that my replies to them must often seem cut and dried. "Oh, she's too opinionated. She's got no sympathy. She's the strong type anyway; she's never agonized as I do. And the way she dishes out advice! Do this, don't do that, trust God, period. I can't handle that stuff." I've heard the objections. I've overheard them, too. In college cafeterias after a talk I've given. At the book table where they're leafing through my books, unaware that the author is sitting to their left, with both ears open.

I thought that if I put these things into a book, they would not seem so cut and dried as they must in a one-page letter. Perhaps I must tell enough of my own story to serve as evidence that I've been there. Could I tell it without stickiness? Without seeming to be at too many removes from people whose vocabulary is different, but whose cries wake clear echoes of my own? I hope I can. But in order to do that I must run the risk of indecent exposure. I must put in my own cries and some of Jim's, my own weaknesses, my falterings—not by any means all (if you knew how much I've left out!), but some samples.

So the book has grown. Letters written to me during the last five or ten years are quoted. My own journals of thirty to thirty-five years ago. Letters from Jim Elliot. Statements as to the principles that apply.

The framework of the book is the story of five and a half years of loving one man, Jim, and of learning the disciplines of longing, loneliness, uncertainty, hope, trust, and unconditional commitment to Christ—a commitment which required that, regardless of what passion we might feel, we must be pure.

It is, to be blunt, a book about virginity. It is possible to love passionately and to stay out of bed. I know. We did it.

Have I nothing to say, then, to those who have already been in bed? I would have to have my head in the sand to imagine that my unmarried readers are all virgins. Those who have given away their virginity write to me, too, some of them in despair, feeling that they are forever banished from purity. I write to them to say that there is no purity in any of us apart from the blood of Jesus. All of us without exception are sinners and sinful, some in one way, some in another. If I can help some to avoid sin, I want to do that. If I can show others that the message of the Gospel is the possibility of a new birth and a new beginning and a new creation, I want to do that.

The love life of a Christian is a crucial battleground. There, if nowhere else, it will be determined as to who is Lord: the world, the self and the devil, or the Lord Christ.

This is why I take the risk. My own love story might be of more or less interest to a few; the "Dear Abby" sort of letters and my replies might be amusing; but my chief concern is that readers consider the authority of Christ over human passion and set their hearts on purity.

In the providence of God, I have had three chances to reflect on and try to practice the principles I write about here. I have been married three times: to Jim Elliot, killed by Indians in the Ecuadorian jungle; to Addison Leitch, killed by cancer; and to Lars Gren, who is feeling fine on the day I'm writing this. Lars has lasted nearly six years, which is longer than either Jim or Add, so he says he is the "front runner." May he outrun me! I will not tell the stories of all three. The Jim Elliot segment should suffice as a framework for what I want to say. Here is a chronology of that segment:

1947—both of us students at Wheaton College, Illinois. He visits our home in New Jersey at Christmas.

1948—Jim confesses his love for me just before I graduate.

Summer, I in Oklahoma, he traveling with a gospel team. No correspondence between us.

Fall, his decision to begin to write to me when I go to Canada to Bible school.

1949—Jim graduates, goes home to Portland, Oregon. I work in Alberta, then visit his home.

1950—Jim at home, working, studying, preparing for missionary work. I in Florida. We spend two days in Wheaton when my brother Dave Howard is married.

1951—We meet again when Jim comes east to speak in missionary meetings in New York and New Jersey.

1952—February, Jim sails for Ecuador. April, I sail for Ecuador. Spend several months in Quito, living with Ecuadorian families to learn Spanish by "immersion."

August, Jim moves to Shandia in the eastern jungle to work with Quichua Indians.

September, I move to San Miguel in the western jungle to work with Colorado Indians.

1953—January, we meet in Quito, Jim asks me to marry him. Engagement announced.

15

June, I move to Dos Rios, eastern jungle, to start study of Quichua, fulfilling the condition of his proposal, "I won't marry you till you learn it."
October 8, married in Quito.
1955—daughter, Valerie, born.
1956—January 8, Jim dies by Auca spears.

(For complete story, see *Through Gates of Splendor, Shadow of the Almighty,* and *The Journals of Jim Elliot.*)

Introduction

On the stack of mail awaiting my return home lay a note saying Lars Gren had called and would I please return the call.

Now, Lars is one of my favorite people, married to another favorite, Elisabeth Elliot. So I called. Elisabeth answered, surprised that Lars had called me, not knowing what it was about.

"Are you working on another book?" I asked Elisabeth. She replied that she just finished one, *Passion and Purity.*

I felt it couldn't be more timely, more on target, and told her I was looking forward to reading it.

When Lars called back—I chuckled to learn, without saying anything to Elisabeth—he wondered if I would be willing to read the manuscript, saying he would understand if I was too busy. When you're that interested in a subject, you feel privileged to get a preview, and I told Lars as much.

Today the manuscript came and I sat down to glance through it.

From the very first it gripped my attention. This wasn't what I expected. Oh, I knew whatever Elisabeth had written would be worth reading and readable, but this is a book about bringing one's love life under the authority and Lordship of Jesus Christ. Elisabeth has made it warmly personal, supporting her theme from memories, journals, and old love letters to Jim Elliot. She writes with poignancy and restraint. Interspersed through it are rich, right words from the Bible, beautiful old hymns, quotations from favorite authors—each so appropriate because they had met a living need. I didn't put it down until I had finished it.

I thought of the confusion of today's young people (and older, alike), Christians as well as non-Christians, and wished everyone could share in Elisabeth and Jim Elliot's love story—a successful (though brief) "orbit into space," because they followed God's guidelines explicitly. "The best way to show up a crooked stick," someone has said, "is to lay a straight one beside it."

So amid today's too-crooked thinking, Elisabeth Elliot Gren has come up with a straight stick. And a beautifully unforgettable one at that.

Ruth Bell Graham

1

Me, Lord? Single?

There was not much of a view from the window. The central feature was the garbage cans behind the dining hall. The closed windows shut out neither the tremendous crash and clatter of early morning collections nor the noisome effluvium of the day's cooking. Nevertheless I was tickled pink to have that little room. It was a single one, what I had been wanting and finally got when I was a senior in college. It had a bed, a bureau, a bookcase, and in the corner by the window, a desk with a straight chair and a lamp. A place for solitude and silence, a "closet" of the sort Jesus said we should go into to pray.

I did my studying and some of my praying at the desk. There were maple trees and an old elm behind the garbage cans, and I was often distracted by the crowd (the flock? the skitter?) of squirrels that lived there. I watched them getting ready for winter, tearing up and down, frantically transporting provisions, scolding, chattering, flicking their tails. I watched the maple leaves change color and fall,

19

watched the rain paste them to the black driveway. I watched snow fall on those trees and cans. It isn't hard at all to put myself back in the chair at that desk. When I sit at a different desk now and read letters from puzzled young people, I become that girl again who gazed out at the snow. What I wore was not very different from what they wear now—styles easily come full circle in thirty-five years. I had two skirts, three sweaters, and a few blouses, which I did my best to mix and match so that it looked as though I was wearing different outfits. Wednesdays were easy. Everybody in the senior class wore the same blue wool blazer with a college emblem sewn over the breast pocket.

My hair gave me an awful time. It was blond, hadn't a hint of a bend in it, and grew about an inch a month. How easy it would have been to wear it hanging long and straight, but that was unthinkable then. My curls were all a "put-up job." I could afford only one permanent a year. In between times I relied on the old pin-curl system, twirling strands of hair around my finger every night before I went to bed, securing them with a bobby pin.

If I couldn't do much with my hair, I could do less with my face. Like most girls, I wished I were pretty, but it seemed futile to tamper much with what I had been given, beyond using a cautious touch of pale lipstick (something called Tangee, which cost ten cents) and a pat of powder on my nose.

I needed that tiny, cozy room that year, perhaps more than ever before. Some issues that would set the sail of my life were to be dealt with. During the preceding summer I had finished praying about whether or not I was to be a missionary. I was. After what my Plymouth Brethren friends would call an exercise and what people now would call a struggle, it was clear at last. The struggle was not over any unwillingness to cross an ocean or live under a thatched roof, but over whether this was my idea or God's and whether I was meant to be a surgeon (I loved dissecting things) or a linguist. I came to the conclusion it was God who called and the call was to linguistics. I asked for assurance from the Lord and got it, so that was that. But there was another matter of business not by any means finished. That was the one for which God knew I would need a "closet." It was about being alone—for the rest of my life. I was saying "Me, Lord? Single?" It seemed to come up between me and my Greek textbooks when I sat at the desk, between me and my Bible when I tried to hear God speaking. It was an obstruction to my prayers and the subject of recurrent dreams.

I talked often about this to God. I don't remember mentioning it to anybody else for many months. The two who shared the suite of which my room was one-third were not the wildly popular sort of whom I would have been envious. They were quiet, sensible girls a few years older than I—one a music major who spent most of her time practicing the organ in the conservatory, the other a former WAVE (the women's branch of the Navy) who was an expert at knitting argyle socks. Both of them, in fact, turned out countless pairs of socks and mittens and sent them off somewhere by parcel post. "When you get a needle in your hand," Jean said to me one day, "you are just lost, aren't you?" Compared to those two, I was.

After college Jean married. Barbara is still single. I have no memory of any discussions with them on love and marriage (though we must have had some), but I am perfectly sure that for all three of us singleness meant one thing: virginity. If you were single, you had not been in bed with any man. If you were to be permanently single, you were never going to be in bed with any man.

That was a hundred years ago, of course. But even a hundred years ago anybody who quite seriously believed that and acted on it would be seen as an oddity by many people. Perhaps we were in the minority. I can't be sure

21

about that. Certainly the majority *professed* to believe that sexual activity was best limited to husbands and wives, whether or not their private lives demonstrated this conviction. Now, however, at the beginning of the twenty-first century, times have changed, they tell us. For thousands of years society depended on some semblance of order in the matter of sex. A man took a wife (or wives) in some regularly prescribed manner and lived with her (or them) according to recognized rules. He "messed around" with other men's wives only to his peril. A woman knew that she possessed a priceless treasure, her virginity. She guarded it jealously for the man who would pay a price for it—commitment to marriage with her and with her alone. Even in societies where polygamy was allowed, rules governed responsibilities to spouses, rules on which the whole stability of the society depended.

Somehow we've gotten the idea that we can forget all the regulations and get away with it. Times have changed, we say. We're "liberated" at last from our inhibitions. We have Sex and the Single Girl now. We have freedom. We can, in fact, "have it all and not get hooked." Women can be predators if they want to, as well as men. Men aren't men unless they've proved it by seducing as many women as possible—or as many men, for we may now choose according to "sexual preference." We can go to bed with those of the opposite sex or those of our own. It doesn't matter. A mere question of taste, and we all have a "right" to our tastes. Everybody's equal. Everybody's free. Nobody is hung up anymore or needs to deny himself anything. In fact, nobody *ought* to deny himself anything he wants badly—it's dangerous. It's unhealthy. It's sick. If it feels good and you don't do it, you're paranoid. If it doesn't feel good and you do do it, you're a masochist.

The reason my roommates and I believed that *singleness* was synonymous with *virginity* was not that we were college students a hundred years ago when everybody believed that. It was not that we didn't know any better. It was not that we were too naïve to have heard that people have been committing adultery and fornication for millennia. It was not that we were not yet liberated or even that we were just plain stupid. The reason is that we were Christians. We prized the sanctity of sex.

I sat at that desk by the window and thought long and hard about marriage. I knew the kind of man I wanted. He would have to be a man who prized virginity—his own as well as mine—as much as I did.

What do women want today? What do men want? I mean, deep down. What do they really want? If "times" have changed, have human longings changed, too? How about principles? Have Christian principles changed?

I say no to the last three questions, an emphatic no. I am convinced that the human heart hungers for constancy. In forfeiting the sanctity of sex by casual, nondiscriminatory "making out" and "sleeping around," we forfeit something we cannot well do without. There is dullness, monotony, sheer boredom in all of life when virginity and purity are no longer protected and prized. By trying to grab fulfillment everywhere, we find it nowhere.

2

The Life I Owe

A young British preacher named Stephen Olford spoke in our college chapel for a week. Two things he said stayed with me: He quoted from the Song of Solomon, "I charge you, O daughters of Jerusalem, that ye stir not up, nor awake love until it please." He interpreted this to mean that no one, man or woman, should be agitated about the choice of a mate, but should be "asleep" as it were, in the will of God, until it should please Him to "awake" him. The other thing he urged was that we should keep a spiritual journal. I determined to follow his advice on both counts.

I bought a small, brown looseleaf notebook, almost exactly the size of my small, brown leather-bound Bible, given to me by my parents for Christmas in 1940. These I kept together at all times. I wrote on the flyleaf of the notebook the Greek words meaning "For to me to live is Christ . . ." On the first page I copied out one stanza of Annie R. Cousin's hymn, taken from the words of Samuel Rutherford:

O Christ, He is the fountain,
The deep, sweet well of love!
The streams on earth I've tasted
More deep I'll drink above:
There to an ocean fulness
His mercy doth expand,
And glory, glory dwelleth
In Immanuel's land.

I called the notebook the "Omer of Manna," taking the idea from Exodus 16:32, "And Moses said, This is the thing which the Lord commandeth, Fill an omer of it to be kept for your generations; that they may see the bread wherewith I have fed you in the wilderness, when I brought you forth from the land of Egypt."

"Lord, what is love?"

. . . God is love; and he that dwelleth in love dwelleth in God. . . .

1 John 4:16

This is my commandment, That ye love one another, as I have loved you.

John 15:12

"Father, how is this possible?"

. . . The love of God is shed abroad in our hearts by the Holy Ghost which is given unto us.

Romans 5:5

O Love, that wilt not let me go,
I rest my weary soul in Thee;
I give Thee back the life I owe,
That in Thine ocean depths its flow
May richer, fuller be.

George Matheson

"I give Thee back the life I owe"—owe? Why owe? It's my life, isn't it?

"Have you forgotten that your body is the temple of the Holy Spirit, who lives in you and is God's gift to you, and that you are not the owner of your own body? You have been bought, and at a price!"

The sense of destiny: Someone has paid for me with blood. How the knowledge lifts my sights beyond the moment's hot desire!

> But now this is the word of the Lord,
> the word of your creator, O Jacob,
> of him who fashioned you, Israel:
> Have no fear: for I have paid your ransom;
> I have called you by name and you are my own.

There my destiny is defined: to be created, fashioned, ransomed, called by name. What was true of Israel is true of the Christian who is a "child of Abraham" by faith.

> When you pass through deep waters, I am with you,
> when you pass through rivers,
> they will not sweep you away;
> walk through fire and you will not be scorched,
> through flames and they will not burn you.
> For I am the Lord your God,
> the Holy One of Israel, your deliverer. . . .

A young woman came to me several years ago to ask, "Is it okay to tell God I'll be a missionary if He'll give me a husband?"

I said no. She had not yet understood His claims. Are we in a bargaining position with our Creator, Redeemer, the Holy One? ". . . It was no perishable stuff, like gold or silver, that bought your freedom from the empty folly of

your traditional ways. The price was paid in precious blood
. . . the blood of Christ."

*March 1, 1948—"So will not we go back from thee: quicken
us, and we will call upon thy name. Turn us again, O Lord God
of hosts, cause thy face to shine; and we shall be saved."*

Psalm 80:18, 19

*On Thy brow we see a thorn-crown,
Blood-drops in Thy track.
O forbid that we should ever
Turn us back.*

Amy Carmichael
"India"

*Lord, I have said the eternal Yes. Let me never, having put my
hand to the plough, look back. Make straight the way of the Cross
before me. Give me love, that there may be no room for a wayward thought or step.*

3

Passion Is a Battleground

The confusion that followed my earnest prayers is not surprising to me now. If there is an Enemy of Souls (and I have not the slightest doubt that there is), one thing he cannot abide is the desire for purity. Hence a man or woman's passions become his battleground. The Lover of Souls does not prevent this. I was perplexed because it seemed to me He should prevent it, but He doesn't. He wants us to learn to use our weapons.

A few samples from my diary of the preceding year illustrate the confusion I was in and provide, I'm afraid, a more accurate sketch of what I was then than memory would lead me to draw.

> *February 2, 1947—Longing for someone to love, but perhaps the Lord wants me only for Himself.*
> *February 3—Sara Teasdale: "Why am I crying after love?"*
> *February 16—Hal dates my roommate, then waits for me later in the evening.*

February 17—Hal walks me home. Don't really want to go out with him.

February 18—Phil asked me out. Refused.

February 21—Hal had five dates with my roommate last week. I haven't had that many with him all told.

February 22—Hal drove me home from the post office. I wrote a poem inspired by the fickleness of couples around me. Should I officially break off with Hal, call for a showdown, just let him work it out?

March 8—Accepted date with Hal for a concert.

March 9—Broke date, told Hal we must stop dating. He said there would never be anyone else.

March 10—Was I hasty?

March 11—Shall I apologize?

March 12—Wished I hadn't broken date.

March 14—Tried to see him.

March 17—Talked, returned presents, thanked him for all he'd done. Miss him.

March 23—Met Jim Elliot. Good talk. Wonderful guy.

July 1—Once in a while I think about singleness . . . God can surely give me abundant life. May I never turn aside.

October 26—Read about Henry Martyn of India, who had to choose between the woman he loved and the mission field. Shall I have to choose between marriage and mission?

October 27—Elizabeth Clephane: "I ask no other sunshine than the sunshine of His face."

November 11—Concerned about future translation work, marriage, teaching Greek next year. My mind not "stayed on Him" (see Isaiah 26:3).

One day a friend in the dormitory asked me how my love life was.

"Love life? But I haven't any."

"Come on. I heard you broke a date with Hal."

"Call that a love life?"

"You know what I mean. You have a choice, at least."

"In a manner of speaking, maybe."

"And didn't I see you out with Phil last week?"

"Phil! You know why *he* asked me."

"No."

"Member of the Bachelor's Club. Has to ask a different girl out every week, preferably one that never gets asked. Flattering, huh?"

Hal, Phil, and a few others. A couple of boys who had shown an interest in me in high school were still around. None of them anything like the husband I was dreaming about.

If times have changed, I see no signs of confusion having lessened. Women still dream and hope, pin their emotions on some man who doesn't reciprocate, and end up in confusion. A girl wrote to me from Texas, pages and pages about how her first love affair had come to nothing and how she then met another, a real dreamboat (or whatever today's equivalent is) named Skip.

> In the brief conversation we had, I knew he was very special. I could tell he had a close walk with the Lord. As my roommate and I were driving home from the supper, she was mumbling something about Skip being real nice, and I was saying to the Lord, "I'll take this one, thank You." Two weeks later he asked me out. It was the fourth of July, and we were going to watch fireworks, but it rained and we ended up in a Little Sambo's, drinking coffee and talking for five hours. When we finally went home, we sat and talked with my roommate and her boyfriend for a while, then Skip asked to see my artwork, and we talked some more. At 2:00 A.M., when we finally decided to call it a day, Skip said "Let's pray." I think it is safe to say that at this point I was definitely hooked. For me this was the beginning of one of the most agonizing experiences I've had. We began dating rather "heavy duty," then Skip began putting it in reverse. It has taken me the last three months to wash him out of my hair. I still love him as much as I ever did, but it doesn't hurt anymore.

The stories get very familiar. In the woman's, always the ancient longing—"And her desire shall be for a husband"—the inextinguishable hope for recognition, response, protection. In the man's story, always the restlessness to wander, experiment, conquer, even though inside there is a:

> hunger not of the belly kind, that's banished with bacon
>   and beans,
> But the gnawing hunger of lonely men for a home and all
>   that it means;
> For a fireside far from the cares that are, four walls and
>   a roof above;
> But oh! so cramful of cozy joy, and crowned with a
>   woman's love.
>
> Robert Service

From the perspective of years, I find it easy to marvel at my own silliness when I was twenty. I listen now to contemporary stories of love hoped for, gained, and lost, and am reminded that it was in these matters of the heart that my own heart was sifted and scoured and exposed, the process of purifying begun.

"Blessed are the pure in heart: for they shall see God."

Must the vision cost so much? Isn't the heart pure enough that has no more than the usual measure of slyness, conscious covetousness, or prurience? Wasn't it sufficient that I honestly desired to love God and do what He wanted?

I have never forgotten the morning when the dean of students, Dr. Charles Brooks, closed his chapel message with the words of an old gospel song. I can still see his humble demeanor, hear his quiet voice:

> One thing I of the Lord desire, for all my life hath miry
>   been—

Be it by water or by fire, Oh, make me clean, Oh, make
    me
    clean!
So wash me now, without, within, or purge with fire, if
    that
    must be,
No matter how, if only sin die out in me, die out in me.

4

Unruly Affections

The Book of Common Prayer contains "collects," which are short prayers comprising ideas gathered or "collected" from the day's reading. The one for the fifth Sunday in Lent is this:

> Almighty God, you alone can bring into order the unruly wills and affections of sinners: Grant your people grace to love what you command and desire what you promise; that, among the swift and varied changes of the world, our hearts may surely there be fixed where true joys are to be found; through Jesus Christ our Lord, who lives and reigns with you and the Holy Spirit, one God, now and forever. Amen.

I had been reading my Bible, I believe, quite faithfully, nearly every day through high school and college. Before that, if I did not always read it myself, I heard it read at home by my father both morning and evening. It took no specially profound understanding of it to know that I did not begin to measure up to its standards. As I grew into womanhood and began to learn what was in my heart I saw very clearly that, of all things difficult to rule, none were more so than my will and affections. They were unruly in the extreme, as the diary entries attest.

Bringing anything at all into order—a messy room, a wild horse, a recalcitrant child—involves some expenditure. Time and energy at least are required. Perhaps even labor, toil, sacrifice, and pain. The answer to the above prayer—the bringing of our unruly wills and affections into order—will cost us something.

> Take my love—my God, I pour
> At Thy feet its treasure store.
>
> Francis Ridley Havergal

It is easy to sing a hymn along with the congregation in church. Many times I had sung that one, not knowing what it would come to mean to me. I do not say I sang it glibly, but my sincerity had to be proved somehow.

There was a student on campus whom I had been noticing more and more since that day in March of my junior year when I had met and talked with him. My brother Dave had been urging me to get acquainted with him ever since then, without much success. He and Dave were on the wrestling squad, so I went to a match, ostensibly to watch Dave. I found myself laughing with the crowd at Jim Elliot, the "India-rubber man," who could be tied in knots but could not be pinned. I noticed Jim in the Foreign Missions Fellowship—earnest, committed to missionary service, outspoken (especially to those who were not particularly concerned about missions). I noticed him standing in dining-hall lines with little white cards in his hand, memorizing Greek verbs or Scripture verses. I heard his name read out semester after semester in the honors convocation. Finally Dave invited Jim to come home to

New Jersey with us for Christmas. We had some long, long talks after the family had gone to bed. The more Jim talked, the more I saw that he fitted the picture of what I hoped for in a husband. He loved to sing hymns, and he knew dozens by heart. He loved to read poetry, loved to read it *aloud.* He was a real man, strong, broadchested, unaffected, friendly, and I thought, very handsome. He loved God. That was the supreme dynamic of his life. Nothing else mattered much by comparison.

He was a Greek major, and so was I. After Christmas I began to hope that he would sit by me in class once in a while. He did. He sat by me often, even when at times he had to trip over other people to get the seat. Was it possible . . . ? Could he be interested . . . ? My hopes rose, but very timidly.

Sunday morning in the dining hall. Because many students went off campus for weekends and many of those who stayed did not get up for breakfast on Sundays, everyone ate in one dining hall instead of three. This was my one chance of the week to see Jim at a meal, since he ate in "Lower Williston," where prices were lower and, we used to say with tongue in cheek, the people humbler. I was sitting with a group of girls in "Upper," just finishing my pancakes, when I glanced toward the door. Jim was coming in. He caught my eye and broke into a wide smile. I floated for the rest of the day. Jim Elliot had smiled at me.

A gospel team trip to Indiana. Jim organized it and chose three men and two women to go along. I was one of them, and we were driving home long after midnight. Jim said he would need somebody to sit beside him who was not sleepy and could talk to keep him awake.

"How 'bout you, Bett?" he said, and my heart turned over. Me, sleepy?

We talked about the day's events, about kids who had responded to our talks on missions, and I suppose other things. I've forgotten. Then Jim recited from memory twenty-one stanzas of Rutherford's hymn, "The Sands of Time Are Sinking." There was "my" verse, the one copied into the Omer of Manna:

"O Christ, He is the fountain, the deep, sweet well of love. . . ."

One night the buzzer sounded on my floor. This meant a phone call downstairs for somebody, but it was hardly ever for me.

"Howard!" somebody shouted. (We often called each other by surnames in those days.)

I raced down to the lounge and picked up the phone.

"Bett? Jim. How 'bout a Coke date over at the Stupe? Like to talk to you."

"Sure. Now?"

"Be right over."

We sat in a booth in the Stupe, nickname for the student recreation center. Jim gave the order, then opened his Bible. I've forgotten the reference, but I remember the talk. It was about my reticence. Jim rebuked me as a "sister in Christ," urged me to be more open, more friendly. Christ could make me freer, if I'd let Him.

I was hurt a little. But I was glad to see Jim's forthrightness, glad I mattered to him, mattered enough for him to speak the truth to me faithfully. Another item on my "checklist"—this was the kind of man I was looking for.

Asking the Lord to give me some form of specific Christian service, I learned that a group of students went regularly to Chicago on Sundays to talk about Christ to people in railroad stations. What could be more daunting?

Remembering Jim's admonitions in the Stupe, I determined not to be daunted. *Do the thing you fear,* I told myself. When I arrived at the Wheaton station to take the train to Chicago the following Sunday afternoon, who should be pacing up and down the platform in the raw wind but Jim Elliot, overcoat flying open, fedora hat at a rakish angle on the back of his head, fat Bible under his arm. Alas. I had no idea he was one of the group. He would surely think I was after him, but I could hardly back down now. None of us took seats together on the train. We hoped for conversation with strangers en route. The fellowship we had as a group was in weekly prayer meetings on campus. One Sunday, the cars being nearly empty on the return trip, Jim threw his Bible onto the seat beside me while he took off his coat and hat. Warmth and chills ran up my spine.

"How did it go, Bett?" he asked. We talked all the way back to Wheaton, and he walked to the dorm with me. Nothing we said has stayed with me except a general impression of encouragement. Maybe he saw that I had chosen what was hardest. He left with a breezy, "See you in Greek class."

Each encounter strengthened the suspicion that I might be falling in love with this man. A delicious feeling, but not very sensible for a woman trying to steer a straight course for the mission field, which, I thought, was supposed to be Africa or the South Seas.

Precisely *how* did one pour at God's feet the "treasure store" of one's love? *Well,* I promised myself, *I'll find out when I really do fall in love. There's no such involvement yet.*

5

Does God Want Everything?

God sifted men's hearts in Old Testament times.

> The time came when God put Abraham to the test. "Abraham," he called, and Abraham replied, "Here I am." God said, "Take your son Isaac, your only son, whom you love, and go to the land of Moriah. There you shall offer him as a sacrifice on one of the hills which I will show you." So Abraham rose early in the morning and saddled his ass . . . and set out. . . .

God was still sifting hearts in New Testament times:

> . . . A man came up and asked him, "Master, what good must I do to gain eternal life?" . . . Jesus said to him, "If you wish to go the whole way, go, sell your possessions, and give to the poor, and then you will have riches in heaven; and come, follow me."

No man is worthy of me who cares more for father or mother than for me; no man is worthy of me who cares more for son or daughter; no man is worthy of me who does not take up his cross and walk in my footsteps. By gaining his life a man will lose it; by losing his life for my sake, he will gain it.

I count everything sheer loss, because all is far out-weighed by the gain of knowing Christ Jesus my Lord, for whose sake I did in fact lose everything. I count it so much garbage, for the sake of gaining Christ.

Great spiritual principles. Unarguable. To all of them, my intellect gave full consent. A giant of the faith like Abraham or Paul the apostle—of course *they* had to be tested with great tests. I was only a college girl, trying to do well in my studies, praying for direction for my life, attracted to a very appealing man whose primary interest was in the Kingdom of God. Anything wrong with that?

"If you wish to go the whole way. . . ." It was not to the intellect alone that the question came. My heart and my feelings were involved now, and I must give an answer. God was sifting *me* this time. Did I want to go the "whole way"? *Yes, Lord.*

"Do you want to be worthy of Me?" *Yes, Lord.*

"Do you want to know Christ Jesus as Lord?" *Certainly, Lord.*

In Lilias Trotter's beautifully illustrated book, *Parables of the Cross,* she describes the death-life cycle of plants, which illustrates the spiritual processes that must go on in us if we are to die to self and live to God. In the love life, as well as in other areas:

The fair new petals must fall, and for no visible reason. No one seems enriched by the stripping.

And the first step into the realm of giving is a like sur-render—not manward but Godward: an utter yielding of our best. So long as our idea of surrender is limited to the renouncing of unlawful things, we have never grasped its true meaning: *that* is not worthy of the name for "no polluted thing" can be offered.

The life lost on the Cross was not a sinful one—the treasure poured forth there was God-given, God-blessed treasure, lawful and right to be kept: only that there was the life of the world at stake.

What kind of a God is it who asks everything of us? The same God who ". . . did not spare his own Son, but gave him up for us all; and with this gift how can he fail to lavish upon us all he has to give?"

He gives all.

He asks all.

April 2—I am seized with fear that my own will will be given place, and I will thus ruin my usableness for God. It would be easy to follow my feelings . . . to interfere with the voice of the Lord when He says, "This is the way, walk ye in it."

I wanted to be loved. Nothing unusual about that, nothing to separate my generation from any other.

But I wanted something deeper. Down among all the foolishness in my diary, thoughts like chaff which the wind of the Spirit can drive away, there was some wheat. There was an honest-to-God longing for the "fixed heart" that the collect speaks of. A thousand questions cluttered my mind, the same ones I find today in the letters I receive. I had thought some of mine were new. My correspondents think the same. They aren't. But the question to precede all others, which finally determines the course of our lives, is What do I really want? Was it to love what God commands, in the words of the collect, and to desire what He promises? Did I want what I wanted, or did I want what He wanted, no matter what it might cost?

Until the will and the affections are brought under the authority of Christ, we have not begun to understand, let alone to accept, His Lordship. The Cross, as it enters the love life, will reveal the heart's truth. My heart, I knew, would be forever a lonely hunter unless settled "where true joys are to be found."

One morning I was reading the story of Jesus' feeding of the five thousand. The disciples could find only five loaves of bread and two fishes. "Let me have them," said Jesus. He asked for all. He took them, said the blessing, and broke them before He gave them out. I remembered what a chapel speaker, Ruth Stull of Peru, had said: "If my life is broken when given to Jesus, it is because pieces will feed a multitude, while a loaf will satisfy only a little lad."

6

The Snake's Reasoning

About two o'clock one morning a few years ago a beautiful girl who was staying in my house knocked on my bedroom door. She had come in from a date and wanted to talk. Sitting down on the end of my bed, she told me of her eagerness to marry a handsome and wealthy man. This was not the man she had just been out with. He was nice enough—a Christian, handsome, interesting, "really neat," but not wealthy.

"What do you want more than anything else in life?" I asked. "God's choices or your own?"

"God's, of course."

"What if He should choose for you a man who was poor and homely?"

"Oh, but He wouldn't!"

"Why not?"

"Because He loves me."

"I see. Then He will give the poor and homely man only to a woman He doesn't love?"

"Oh, but—"

"Or—think about this one—does He love the poor, homely man? If so, will He give him an ugly woman? Or might He give him a beautiful one?"

"Oh, please!"

"You said you wanted God's choices, Jane, and God's choices involve His plans for a whole universe—all the atoms, all the worlds, all the people, pretty and ugly, rich and poor. He's engineering an intricate pattern for good, and part of that pattern might necessitate giving a beautiful girl to a homely man. Maybe the man with no looks and no money is praying God will give you to him. What about *that*, now?"

"That's too complicated for me. I've prayed for His will, and I've prayed for a rich, handsome husband, and that's what I'm going to get, because Jesus loves me and Jesus wants me to be happy."

"So if you don't get him, will that prove God doesn't love you?"

The blue eyes filled with tears. "Doesn't He want me to be happy?" (I heard an echo of Eve in Eden.)

"He wants you most to be holy."

"Miserable and long faced, then. Is that what God wants? Is that what holiness has to mean?"

"Has to? No. Not only doesn't have to, but can't. Real holiness can't possibly be miserable and long faced, Jane. *Holiness* means 'wholeness.' Comes from the same root as *hale*—you know, hale and hearty. Healthy. Fulfilled."

"Well, that has to mean happy."

"That's what it means for sure. The problem starts when we make up our own minds what will give us happiness and then decide, if we don't get exactly that, that God doesn't love us. We slither into a slough of God-hates-me self-pity."

"But you just said He wants us to be happy. He must want to give us what we want, doesn't He? I mean, within reason."

"He wanted Adam and Eve to be happy, but He didn't give them everything they wanted. He knew it would be the death of them. So they got mad and decided He didn't love them and was being stingy when He told them not to touch the fruit. How could He love them if He didn't let them have it? They put more stock in the snake's reasoning than in God's."

A slip of paper handed to me at a seminar had this question written on it: "What do you do when you feel you've come to a point that your singlehood appears to be an inadequate status for deep personal growth? How long do you hang on?"

Good thing I wasn't on the platform when that question came. I might have chuckled. I toyed with the idea of giving a facetious answer: "Three more days, then go out and either ask somebody to marry you or hang yourself."

But of course that was not what I said. The crux of the matter is that phrase "an inadequate status for deep personal growth." Is that what singleness is? Does that mean that marriage and only marriage is an adequate status for deep personal growth? How ever did Jesus manage, then, as a single man?

I'm afraid the snake has been talking to that person. He's been sneaking up and whispering, "God is stingy. He dangles that beautiful fruit called marriage before your eyes and won't let you have it. He refuses you the only thing you need for deep personal growth, the one thing in all the world that would solve all your problems and make you really happy."

7

The First Date

The first date Jim asked me for was to a missionary meeting at Moody Church in Chicago, late in April. Not surprising that he would choose an event like this rather than a concert or dinner out. The speaker was one of the daughters of the famous missionary to Africa C. T. Studd. She told of her father's last hours. He lay on his cot, gazing around the little hut and at his few possessions. "I wish I had something to leave to each of you," he said to the handful of people present, "but I gave it all to Jesus long ago."

May 1, 1948—Today has been one of a strong testing. A letter came in the intercollege mail, which brought me to my knees. How graciously the Lord gave 1 John 1:7, ". . . if we walk in the light as he himself is in the light, then we share together a common life, and we are being cleansed from every sin by the blood of Jesus his Son." Hold me steadily in Thy way, for I am Thy servant.

May 2—Spent all morning with God. Raining too hard to walk to church. It is hard to know how to deal with this new thing. I

am willing to do God's will, but I cannot tell if my desires are wrong and should be "plucked out."
May 3—Today there was a complete committal to God.

The letter, of course, was from Jim. He confessed to having been in some way out of line on the evening of our date. It was a bit obscure to me, but I felt I might have been at fault. "This new thing" was the strong feeling suddenly awakened just when I had thought I was learning how to be "asleep" in the will of God. I was very much awake.

The Lord told King David to set up an altar on the threshing floor that belonged to Araunah the Jebusite. When the king asked Araunah if he might buy it, Araunah begged him to take it, as a gift, along with his oxen for an offering and the threshing sledges for fuel. "No," said the king, ". . . I will not offer to the Lord my God whole-offerings that have cost me nothing. . . ."

Lord, I said, *here's my heart.*

May 4—More testing today. God is asking me insistently, "Lovest thou Me?" and I find myself evading the question. Then comes the answer, Yes, Lord. I'm conscious of the warring of the flesh and spirit—the spirit willing, the flesh weak. Evidently I need the test.

Hold Thou Thy cross between us, blessed Lord.
Let us love Thee. To us Thy power afford
To remain prostrate at Thy pierced feet—
There is no other place where we may meet.

Set Thou our faces as a flint of stone
To do Thy will. Our goal be this alone.
O God, our hearts are fixed. Let us not turn.
Consume all our affections, let Thy love burn.

May 5—Jim and I studied together as we usually do on Mondays, Wednesdays, and Fridays.

May 6—Who would have guessed what a few days would bring forth? How can God work His will in me if I am clogged with wishes of my own? Thy will be done.

I was certainly in a state! "Clogged with wishes." I was wishing that my wishes were what God wished, and if my wishes were not what God wished, I wished that I could wish that my wishes would go away, but the wishes were still there.

May 9—From the best bliss that earth imparts
  We turn unfilled to Thee again.
  "Jesus, Thou Joy of Loving Hearts"
May 12—Jim Elliot was elected president of Foreign Missions Fellowship for next year.

8

Unfailing Love

"But how in the world can I find out what God wants me to do, if I don't know what *I* want to do?" The logic of this question escapes me, but it is one I have heard more than once. Why not start by simply telling God you'll do anything He says? You're the servant. He's the master. It's the only reasonable approach, isn't it? Furthermore, there *is* the possibility that what He says will be something you'd like.

Speaking of teenagers of the eighties, Joan Schuman, director of Massachusetts' Bureau of Student Services, said, "It is their selfishness that strikes me most of all. The predominant theme is 'What's in it for me?' and 'I don't care what happens to my fellowman.'"

There are over a million pregnancies per year among unmarried girls under twenty. This seems to illustrate Miss Schuman's observation. What they want they take, any way they can get it. Where do they learn this? Some of them, sadly, from their parents, who have shed the responsibility of marriage, home, and children for another "lifestyle," another partner, another career, another bid for the happiness that will always elude them. If a mother or father, by behavior, says in effect, "It's my life, this is what I want, the rest of you be damned," their children will follow suit. Who shows them another way?

It would be foolish to deny that there are some pleasures along that road. There is plenty of what people call fun. There are thrills, gratifications, "experiences."

A road may seem straightforward to a man,
yet may end as the way to death.
Even in laughter the heart may grieve,
and mirth may end in sorrow.

There is another way: to love what God commands and desire what He promises. It can't be found except through prayer and obedience. It cuts quite across the other way, takes us where things are not at the mercy of changing fashions and opinions. It is a place where a man's heart may safely rest—and a woman's heart, too.

1 Peter 5:7 (NEB): *"Cast all your cares on him, for you are his charge."*

Philippians 4:6 (NEB): *". . . Have no anxiety, but in everything make your requests known to God. . . ."*

Matthew 6:25 (NEB): *". . . I bid you put away anxious thoughts. . . ."*

merimna—*"care, thought, disquietude, trouble."*

merimnao—*"be anxious, be cumbered, think earnestly upon."*

The journal does not say what was troubling me the day I copied the above verses and looked up the operative Greek words. It is manifest that the anxiety that shadowed too many of my days was that I should miss the path of righteousness. Better *that* anxiety, perhaps, than a cavalier carelessness, but the years since have proved to me

49

over and over again that the heart set to do the Father's will need never fear defeat. His promises of guidance may be fully counted upon. Does it make sense to believe that the Shepherd would care less about getting His sheep where He wants them to go than they care about getting there?

I will teach you, and guide you in the way you should go.
I will keep you under my eye.
Do not behave like horse or mule, unreasoning creatures, whose course must be checked with bit and bridle.
    Many are the torments of the ungodly;
but unfailing love enfolds him who trusts in the Lord.
Rejoice in the Lord and be glad. . . .

9

The Revelation

A settled commitment to the Lord Christ and a longed-for commitment to Jim Elliot seemed to be in conflict. Discipleship usually brings us into the necessity of choice between duty and desire. They are not always mutually exclusive, however. When our hearts are set on obedience, we can be sure of the needed wisdom to tell the difference between a conflict and a harmony. It may be a slow and painful process.

On Memorial Day the missions fellowship had a picnic breakfast at a place called the Lagoon. When it was over, I was one of those helping to clean up. Jim was another, and of course I kept him somewhere in the corner of my eye. When everything was finished, I looked up to see him sitting on a picnic table, with two friends. Bill and Van were talking; Jim was swinging his legs and gazing at me. Everybody else had gone. He jumped off the table and ran over to where I was dumping the last load into a trash barrel.

"Walk you home?"

"Okay. Bill and Van coming?"

"They're deep into something. Let's leave 'em alone."

We walked half a block in silence. Then, suddenly, "We've got to get squared away on how we feel about each other," Jim said. I was dumbfounded. No preliminaries, nothing. Just like that. Bang. The revelation I'd been hoping for—he *had* some feelings. And he was assuming that I had some. I was a little piqued at this assumption. It seemed presumption, since I thought I had done quite well at concealing my interest. The last thing I wanted was to hint in any way that I had thought twice about him—until, that is, he hinted that he was interested in me. Now what was I to say?

"Feel about each other? You mean—"

"Come on, Bett. Don't tell me you didn't know I was in love with you?"

"I had no idea."

"Really? But you must have! If you didn't—then all I can say is you must have thought I was a pretty nice guy. I've been knocking myself out to be near you, be nice to you, show you how I felt without actually saying anything. You mean you didn't notice?"

"I noticed. I was afraid to believe my eyes. I told myself you couldn't possibly be interested, let alone—"

"In love. That's what I'm telling you. Hey, we're not going to campus now. Let's go back to the Lagoon and talk this thing out."

Seven hours later, sunburned, floating in a rainbow haze, we said good-bye on the front steps of my dormitory. I went up to my room, glad for that little "closet" to think in.

Rainbows are made of sunlight and rain. The sunlight, which turned my world into a radiance of color, was the knowledge of Jim Elliot's love. The rain was the other fact he explained to me as we sat on the grass by the Lagoon— that God was calling him to remain single. Perhaps for life, perhaps only until he had had firsthand experience in the place where he was to work as a jungle missionary. Older missionaries had told him that single men were needed to do jobs married ones could never do. There were some areas where women could not go. Jim took their word for it and committed himself to bachelorhood for as long as the will of God required.

June 3—"Whom have I in heaven but thee? and there is none upon earth that I desire beside thee."

Psalm 73:25

"Arise ye, and depart; for this is not your rest. . . ."

Micah 2:10

"And the Lord spake unto Aaron, Thou shalt have no inheritance in their land . . . I am thy part and thine inheritance . . ."

Numbers 18:20

". . . She went after her lovers, and forgat me, saith the Lord."

Hosea 2:13

"I will even betroth thee unto me in faithfulness: and thou shalt know the Lord."

Hosea 2:20

"I have set the Lord always before me . . ."

Psalm 16:8

"Thou wilt shew me the path of life . . ."

Psalm 16:11

"Hold up my going in thy paths, that my footsteps slip not."

Psalm 17:5

I was very cautious about what I put in the journals. I don't think it was because I feared someone else would discover my secrets. I think I was afraid to articulate, even for myself, feelings I might have to get rid of. Better to stick with what God was saying to me than what my heart was saying. It seemed the safer course. I do not repudiate it now. The only way to build a house on the rock is to *hear* the Word (I couldn't have heard it if all I listened to was my feelings) and then to try to do it. The collection of verses in the above journal entry represents warnings and aspirations that shaped my thinking. Admittedly they are not in context, but I believe God gave them to me to show certain aspects of the truth at the time. The Holy Spirit was given to guide us into all truth, but He doesn't do it all at once.

10

Does God Notice?

Thou shalt know Him when He comes
Not by any din of drums,
Nor the vantage of His airs,
Nor by anything He wears,
Neither by His crown nor His gown.
For His presence known shall be
By the holy harmony
Which His coming makes in thee.

In the days following our talk at the Lagoon I prayed for that holy harmony. It seemed impossible that the torrent of passion could be brought into the calm river of God's purposes for Jim or for me, but I prayed for it anyway.

We had sat on the grass by the lake and talked of how each had agonized over the question of singleness, knowing that our chances of finding a mate in missionary work would be strictly limited. Jim said he had no intention of looking for one. He had found the one he wanted.

"If I marry, I know who it'll be. That is, of course, if she'll have me." He flashed his famous smile. I smiled in reply. He hastened to add, "But I'm not asking. I can't do that, Bett, and you'll have to understand that. I can't ask you to marry me, and I can't ask you to commit yourself to anything whatever. I can't even ask you to wait. I've given you and all my feelings for you to God. He'll have to work out whatever He wants."

Could He? My mind was full of questions. I thanked God for a man who put Him first. I could not have gotten terribly excited about one whose spiritual hunger did not parallel my own. But Jim was not just spiritual. He was very physical. He had a wrestler's build—strong neck, barrel chest, muscular arms and legs. He had brown hair, fair skin, blue eyes, beautiful teeth, and a good square jaw.

"I'm hungry for you, Bett," he had said. He was not one to beat about the bush. "We're alike in our desire for God. I'm glad for that. But we're different, too. I've got the body of a man, and you've got the body of a woman, and frankly, I want you. But you're not mine."

Not his. God's. That much was clear. But what was God going to do about all this? Was He interested in the plight of two college kids? Had our cause perhaps escaped His notice? Would He bother with us, when He was busy with who knew how many worlds?

> Who had gauged the waters in the palm of his hand,
>   or with its span set limits to the heavens?
> Who has held all the soil of earth in a bushel,
>   or weighed the mountains on a balance
>   and the hills on a pair of scales? . . .
> Do you not know, have you not heard,
>   were you not told long ago,
>   have you not perceived ever since the world began,
>   that God sits throned on the vaulted roof of earth,
>   whose inhabitants are like grasshoppers? . . .

> Lift up your eyes to the heavens;
> consider who created it all,
> led out their host one by one
> and called them all by their names;
>> through his great might, his might and power,
>> not one is missing.

Not a star, not a planet, not a meteorite or a quasar, no, not even a black hole or a black dwarf is missing. God made them. He knows their names, knows exactly where they belong. Can He keep track of us?

> Why do you complain, O Jacob,
>> and you, Israel, why do you say,
> "My plight is hidden from the Lord,
> and my cause has passed out of God's notice"?
> Do you not know, have you not heard?
> The Lord, the everlasting God, creator of the wide world,
>> grows neither weary nor faint;
>> no man can fathom his understanding.
> He gives vigour to the weary,
> new strength to the exhausted.
> Young men may grow weary and faint,
> even in their prime they may stumble and fall;
> but those who look to the Lord will win new strength,
> they will grow wings like eagles;
> they will run and not be weary,
> they will march on and never grow faint.

11

Oozing Ache

June 1, 1948—The sun shone, and I sent a copy of a poem to Jim.

June 2—"the dust of words is cumbersome" (Jim).

June 3—Jim gave me a beautiful little leather-bound hymnbook with the flyleaf inscribed, "To Betty, '. . . I will sing with the spirit, and I will sing with the understanding also. . . . Speaking . . . in spiritual songs . . . singing. . . . Giving thanks . . .' (1 Corinthians 14:15, Ephesians 5:19, 20). May He show us more of' τὰ περὶ εαυτου ' (Luke 24:27). Jim."

June 4—Terribly difficult to study. Could not get to sleep. Could not eat much breakfast.

On June 6 Jim wrote these lines:

> O Lord, against this bosom blast
>   of coiled and seething feelings,
> Batt'ring passions, ebbing yearnings,
>   oozing ache of inner man,
> Raise Thou the flinty walls of stuff of
>   which Thy Son was made.
> Yea, build in me the buttressed
>   bastions of faith

> That shall resist the undersucking flow
> of soulish tide,
> And make me to endure this late attack,
> I pray, in Jesus' name.

On the next evening we took a long walk, talking about the "codes" each of us had built, Jim on Matthew 19:12, "For while some are incapable of marriage because they were born so, or were made so by men, there are others who have themselves renounced marriage for the sake of the kingdom of Heaven. Let those accept it who can." Jim put himself in the last category. He was prepared to renounce marriage if that was necessary in his case in order to obey God. As far as he knew, he was able to accept that, at least for now. My code came from Isaiah 54:5, "Your husband is your maker, whose name is the Lord of Hosts," and from 1 Corinthians 7:34, 35, "The unmarried or celibate woman cares for the Lord's business; her aim is to be dedicated to him in body as in spirit; but the married woman cares for worldly things; her aim is to please her husband. In saying this I have no wish to keep you on a tight rein. I am thinking simply of your own good, of what is seemly, and of your freedom to wait upon the Lord without distraction."

No Christian ought to put himself outside the possibility that this is his assignment. The claims must be considered. Jim and I were startled to find how closely in this, as in other matters, our thoughts seemed to coincide. We cautioned each other about the dangers of being taken by such coincidence. More sins are defended by the claim of coincidence ("it was meant to be") than this world dreams of—or at least than it admits. We decided the best thing to do was pray steadily and wait patiently till God made the way plain.

12

Holding Pattern

I began to learn to wait. Patient waiting does not come naturally to most of us, but a great deal is said about it in the Bible. It is an important discipline for anyone who wants to learn to trust.

> *June 9, 1948—"Lead me in thy truth, and teach me: for thou art the God of my salvation; on thee do I wait all the day."*
>
> Psalm 25:5

> *To wait on the Lord is to stand perfectly still. . . . Can we two trust His words, "Is not the Lord your God with you? and hath he not given you rest on every side? . . ."*
>
> 1 Chronicles 22:18

> *Last night I read chapter 43 in* Windows *by Amy Carmichael: "Bare heights of loneliness . . . a wilderness whose burning winds sweep over glowing sands, what are they to Him? Even there He can refresh us, even there He can renew us."*

It was on the evening of the same day, June 9, that Jim and I walked out to a cemetery and sat down on a stone slab. I told him I did not think it would help us much in discerning God's direction if we started right in on a heavy correspondence. Wouldn't it make more sense to "cool it"? Not that we used that expression in those days, but it says what I meant. To allow for the perspective that both distance and silence could give might help us to see the whole thing with cool reason.

Jim thought that over for a few minutes. Then he spoke of the story he had read in his Bible study that morning—the story of Abraham's offering up of the most precious thing in his life: his son Isaac. "So I put you on the altar," he said.

Slowly we became aware that the moon, which had risen behind us, was casting the shadow of a stone cross on the slab between us.

We were silent for a very long time, pondering this undeniable sign. What Abraham did was the ancient prelude to the full revelation of the love of God. The readiness to give up his son and the rewards promised because of it—again, the central truth of the Cross was brought to us in a strange and mysterious manner. When the silence became heavy, Jim said, "And what is to be done with the ashes?" Time would show.

A girl wrote to me recently, "It seems that time and patience are such key elements to following the way we were intended to go. I think with a good deal of awe upon the fact that you and your first husband waited so long in such careful seeking of obedience, and I wonder, with a lack of knowing inside, whether that is what is required."

I could not tell her that the same duration of waiting was required of her. She will have to take Christ's yoke upon her and learn of Him. I do know that waiting on God requires the willingness to bear uncertainty, to carry within oneself the unanswered question, lifting the heart to God about it whenever it intrudes upon one's thoughts. It is easy to talk oneself into a decision that has no permanence—easier sometimes than to wait patiently.

> Truly my heart waits silently for God;
> my deliverance comes from him.
> In truth he is my rock of deliverance,
> my tower of strength, so that I stand unshaken. . . .
> Trust always in God, my people,
> pour out your hearts before him;
> God is our shelter.

A roof over our heads. A hedge. A windbreak. A warm coat. Shelter from the fear of loss of this precious thing called love, from the fear of a life of loneliness without the one person I believed I could ever love. Shelter from attack—from onslaughts of doubt that God would take care of everything if I would simply trust Him—what if He didn't?

Waiting *silently* is the hardest thing of all. I was dying to talk to Jim and about Jim. But the things that we feel most deeply we ought to learn to be silent about, at least until we have talked them over thoroughly with God.

In *Idylls of the King,* when King Arthur asked Sir Bors if he had seen the Holy Grail, Bors said, "'Ask me not, for I may not speak of it; I saw it;' and the tears were in his eyes."

Luke tells us in his Gospel that, when Jesus was teaching every day in the temple, He went off to spend every night on the Mount of Olives. The words He had for the people came out of prolonged silence on that quiet hillside, away from the city, under the silent stars.

Three days before my graduation, Jim and I spent the afternoon in a little park in Glen Oak, Illinois. We talked very little, enjoyed the sun, flowers, lake, birds, and insects.

I am sure my heart was full to bursting with things I wanted to say (things like, "I love you, I can't live without you. How can you do this? I can't bear it," and all the rest of the desperate phrases women always want to say). I refrained, but it was all I could do. I am sure it was good for me to refrain. "Never pass up an opportunity to keep your mouth shut" is a good rule that harmonizes with Scripture, ". . . Keep your mouth shut and show your good sense." ". . . The man who talks too much meets his deserts," and "When men talk too much, sin is never far away; common sense holds its tongue." Finding a mutual appreciation of sun, lake, and birds was a safe kind of communication for us that afternoon. God's time for further revelations of the heart might come later. Tomorrow was not our business; it was His. Letting it rest with Him was the discipline for the day, and it was enough.

"Do you think God will let me know once and for all whether He is going to give me a husband? I'm in a holding pattern, it seems, and I'd like to know how long it's to go on." That is from a letter I received in 1982, but it could have been written by me in 1948. It's exactly how I felt. "If only God would let me know." But then, of course, there was the possibility that He was not going to give me a husband. Did I want to know *that?* Was I ready for it? Perhaps it was better to hope than to know. The "holding pattern" seems to describe a very important aspect of waiting on God. Most of us who travel by air have experienced this. The flight is nearly over, the plane has begun its descent toward the city of destination when you feel it pull up again, bank, and begin to circle. An announcement comes over the intercom, "Ladies and gentlemen, this is your captain speaking. Due to heavy incoming traffic, the tower has assigned us a holding pattern." People groan. Babies cry. You look out and see the same scenery you saw fifteen minutes earlier. You think of the person waiting at the airport for you. You look at your watch and try to figure what will happen if you don't make your connection or appointment. You hope the captain will tell you exactly how long it will be before landing. How long is this circling going to go on? S. D. Gordon, in his *Quiet Talks on Prayer,* describes waiting. It means:

> Steadfastness, that is holding on;
> patience, that is holding back;
> expectancy, that is holding the face up;
> obedience, that is holding one's self in readiness to go or
>   do;
> listening, that is holding quiet and still so as to hear.

How long, Lord, must I wait?
Never mind, child. Trust Me.

13

Material for Sacrifice

A couple of days remained before Jim and I were to part. My family came for my graduation, and I had to make choices between going to various events with them or going for a walk with Jim. Sometimes they won. Sometimes he did. One more trip to the Lagoon. "It's going to be hard," he said. "Harder than we'd like to think." Then the next night, a Sunday, no time for a long walk to the Lagoon. Only a field near the campus, where we sat on a blanket while dew fell and ruined my hair. "Man, your hair sure went straight!" he said, just when I was hoping he would not notice. I think this evening was the first time Jim touched me. He ran the back of his finger down my cheek. A small gesture, big with meaning. I thought of it a thousand times afterwards.

The verses in the *Daily Light* that day were, "Every thing that may abide the fire, ye shall make it go through the fire. . . . The Lord your God proveth you, to know whether ye love the Lord your God with all your heart and with all your soul. . . . Thou, O God, hast proved us: thou hast tried us, as silver is tried." Purity comes at a high price. There was no getting away from that. It seemed that every book I picked up reminded me of the same spiritual principle.

What has been like water from the well of Bethlehem to you recently? Love, friendship, spiritual blessing? Then at the peril of your soul you take it to satisfy yourself. If you do, you cannot pour it out before the Lord. How am I to pour out spiritual gifts, or natural friendship, or love? How can I give them to the Lord? In one way only—in the determination of the mind, and that takes about two seconds. If I hold spiritual blessings or friendship for myself they will corrupt me, no matter how beautiful they are. I have to pour them out before the Lord, give them to Him in my mind, though it looks as if I am wasting them, even as David poured the water out on the sand, to be instantly sucked up.

Chambers's reference is to the story of David's sudden longing, when he was hiding from his enemies in the cave of Adullam, for a drink of water from the well of Bethlehem. Three of his men risked their lives to pass through the Philistines' line and get it for him. David poured it out on the ground, refusing to "drink the blood" of his men.

God gives us material for sacrifice. Sometimes the sacrifice makes little sense to others, but when offered to Him is always accepted. What was the "point" in God's asking Abraham for the sacrifice of his beloved son, Isaac? The story has often been attacked as "pagan" and has been grossly misunderstood. Our offerings to Him may very likely be seen as senseless or even fanatical, but He receives them. Jesus received the precious ointment from the worshiping woman, although those present thought it a foolish waste. It is a lesson I understood very dimly in 1948, but it has become clearer and clearer the further I go with God. I have tried to explain it sometimes to people who are lonely and longing for love. "Give it to Jesus," I say.

The loneliness itself is material for sacrifice. The very longings themselves can be offered to Him who understands perfectly. The transformation into something He can use for the good of others takes place only when the offering is put into His hands.

What will He do with these offerings? Never mind. He knows what to do.

Graduation was in the morning. In the afternoon Jim drove me to the railroad station in Chicago to catch the *Texas Chief*. I wanted him to kick over all the traces, grab me in a rib-cracking embrace, and kiss me without taking a breath till the train started to pull away. That was what one part of me wanted. Another part said no.

It was a long night en route to Oklahoma. Springfield, Kansas City, Wichita. How many stops in between? I woke at each, trying to calculate how far I was from Jim now, picturing him sleeping soundly (dreaming, perhaps?) in the guest room of his aunt's house, where he was to spend several weeks before going home to Oregon. I had copied a poem by Alice Meynell in a notebook. I took it out from time to time, until I had it memorized:

> Let this goodbye of ours, this last goodbye,
> Be still and splendid like a forest tree . . .
> Let there be one grand look within our eyes
> Built of the wonderment of the past years,
> Too vast a thing of beauty to be lost
> In quivering lips and burning floods of tears.

At least Jim hadn't seen the quivering lips or the tears. After we shook hands (clasped hands would be more accurate), he stood there while I walked down the platform, almost the whole length of the train, to the car where my seat was. I waved to him in the distance as I boarded.

14

Honor Above Passion

Does the story seem strange? Does it stretch to the breaking point an early twenty-first century credulity? If it does, perhaps it is because there is an idea of honor here that has largely been lost. Honor is fidelity to a system of fixed values and relations. Is there anything today, even in the imagination of the Christian, for which we are willing to pay the price of self-sacrifice? Any ideal left, any clear-cut goal, any control of passion? Surely there is somewhere, but it is hard to find. Richard Lovelace wrote of it in the seventeenth century, in his poem "To Lucasta, Going to the Wars":

> Tell me not, sweet, I am unkind,
>   That from the nunnery
> Of thy chaste breast and quiet mind
>   To war and arms I fly. . . .
> I could not love thee, dear, so much,
>   Loved I not honor more.

I write in the hope that those who know what honor means will be cheered to see that they are not entirely alone. It may strengthen them to find that, even in recent decades, there are those who recognize something far greater than their own passions, even though for the world at large there seems to be nothing else of any consequence. The majority will sacrifice anything—security, honor, self-respect, the welfare of people they love, obedience to God—to passion. They will even tell themselves that they are obeying God (or at least that He doesn't mind) and congratulate themselves for being so free, so released, so courageous, so honest, and "up front."

The greater the potential for good, the greater the potential for evil. That is what Jim and I found in the force of the love we bore for each other. A good and perfect gift, these natural desires. But so much the more necessary that they be restrained, controlled, corrected, even crucified, that they might be reborn in power and purity for God.

I don't think we ever talked about honor as a concept. Jim honored me as a woman; I honored him as a man. We saw the difference, all right. How sharply we saw and felt and were awed by the difference between a man and a woman. A system of fixed values and relations held us apart, each holding the other in reverence for the Owner. His we were, all the rights were His, all the prerogatives to give or to withhold according to the pattern of His will, which remained as yet a mystery to us. Few, I suppose, even of those who hold the same system of values, need to go through so prolonged and so exquisitely cautious a process. Perhaps most learn their lessons with greater facility than we did. I don't know. For us, this was the way we had to walk, and we walked it, Jim seeing it his duty to protect me, I seeing it mine to wait quietly, not to attempt to woo or entice.

The constraints of godly love are beautifully expressed by Christina Rossetti:

Trust me, I have not earned your dear rebuke,—
   I love, as you would have me, God the most;
   Would lose not Him, but you, must one be lost,
Nor with Lot's wife cast back a faithless look,
Unready to forego what I forsook;
   This say I, having counted up the cost,
   This, though I be the feeblest of God's host,
The sorriest sheep Christ shepherds with His crook.
Yet while I love my God the most, I deem
   That I can never love you over-much;
   I love Him more, so let me love you too;
   Yea, as I apprehend it, love is such
I cannot love you if I love not Him,
   I cannot love Him, if I love not you.

15

Little Deaths

The University of Oklahoma, where I studied linguistics, has an enormous stadium. Nothing was happening there during the summer, so I often climbed to the top row of bleachers, following supper, to enjoy whatever breeze there might be after the day's scorching heat, and to watch those sensational Oklahoma sunsets. It was a lovely place to be alone to think, read, and pray.

I was disturbed to find that I could not think, read, or pray except about Jim Elliot. He loomed in every thought, every line I read in the Bible or anywhere else. He got mixed up in the morphology, syntax, and phonetics I was stuffing into my head. He distracted my prayers. It is a good thing the Lord has compassion on all who fear Him, knows how we are made, and remembers we are only dust. He loved us both, knew exactly how we loved each other, and used even the detours to bring us home again. Someone once observed that the toothache you have this very minute is the worst pain in the world. Lovesickness may seem a trifle compared with other maladies, but the one who is sick with love is sick indeed, and the Heavenly Father understands that. He steadily draws us along the pathway to glory, if our deepest heart is set on His kingdom, if we are not of those whom Psalm 78:8 describes as "a generation with no firm purpose, with hearts not fixed steadfastly on God."

> *July 3—Psalm 44:18, 19* [NEB]: *"We have not gone back on our purpose, nor have our feet strayed from thy path. Yet thou hast crushed us as the sea-serpent was crushed and covered us with the darkness of death."*

> *I wait.*
> *Dear Lord, Thy ways*
> *Are past finding out,*
> *Thy love too high.*
> *O hold me still*
> *Beneath Thy shadow.*
> *It is enough that Thou*
> *Lift up the light*
> *Of Thy countenance.*
> *I wait—*
> *Because I am commanded*
> *So to do. My mind*
> *Is filled with wonderings.*
> *My soul asks "Why?"*
> *But then the quiet word,*
> *"Wait thou only*
> *Upon God."*
> *And so, not even for the light*
> *To show a step ahead,*
> *But for Thee, dear Lord,*
> *I wait.*

Jim's brother Bert was a student at the university with me. In chapel sometimes I would suddenly catch a glimpse of his profile—so like Jim's. After supper we would take turns playing the piano and teaching each other favorite hymns in the dining hall. He sang as Jim sang—heartily, unabashedly, a good man's voice with no affectations. His presence was a constant reminder of Jim.

"When the will of God crosses the will of man," Addison Leitch said, "somebody has to die." Life requires countless "little" deaths—occasions when we are given the chance to say no to self and yes to God. The Apostle Paul said, "For continually, while still alive, we are being surrendered into the hands of death, for Jesus' sake. . . ." It is not that everything that has anything to do with ourselves is in itself wicked and deserving of death. It did not mean that when Jesus said, "Not my will. . . ." There could not have been even the smallest part of His will that was wicked. It was a choice to lay down everything—the good He had done and the good He might do if He was permitted to live—for the love of God. The same choice is offered to us. The see Bert's profile, hear him sing; to contemplate the blessedness of marriage as I watched couples who were taking the same course at the university; to call up in memory the sweet anguish of those hours by the Lagoon; to picture Jim's face as we said good-bye at Union Station—only "little deaths," but little deaths have to be died just as great ones do. Every reminder that aroused a longing had to be offered up.

There is a big *however*. It is this: We are not meant to die merely in order to be dead. God could not want that for the creatures to whom He has given the breath of life. *We die in order to live.*

A seed falls into the dark earth and dies. Out of its death comes multiplied life. As Saint Francis prayed, "It is in giving that we receive, it is in pardoning that we are pardoned, it is in dying that we are born to eternal life."

It takes faith to believe this, as it takes faith for a farmer to plant a seed. It takes faith to live by it, faith to act on it, faith to keep looking at the joyful end of it all. A failure of faith here leads certainly to resentment and then to depression. The destruction will go on and on.

16

Life From Death

July 4, Oklahoma—Spent another of those long and glorious evenings in the sunset, at the top of the stadium. There in prayer and meditation, I learned three things.

1. There was a tiny scrap of rainbow—just an end of ribbon in the clouds—and I knew that it was for me. It was a promise of good things. I could not see the other end, nor the great sweeping arc that reached high above the clouds that shadowed me, but I could see that bit and knew it spoke of His faithfulness, for He is faithful that promised.

2. Then there came some clouds of pure gold. There was nothing in those clouds to make them gold—only mist. Neither is there anything in my cloud to make it shine—perhaps a mist of tears, nothing else. But the Sun has lifted up His light. The Lord made His face to shine on me and was gracious to me, and gave me peace, there in the evening sunset.

3. He gave the words, ". . . Except a corn of wheat fall into the ground and die, it abideth alone: but if it die, it bringeth forth much fruit" (John 12:24). So it was with our little kernel of possibility. So small, but buried. And I asked God to water it, there in its darkness, and transform the dead thing into fruit. What fruit will He bring forth? If only it could be that from so small a seed He might create the fruits of the Spirit in me, even just the beginning of learning of them: love, joy, peace, long-suffering, gentleness, goodness, faith, meekness, temperance.

O Great Giver of Harvest:
Show us the grain, the golden harvest there
For corn of wheat that [we] have buried here.

Amy Carmichael
"Toward Jerusalem"

July 5. The sunset tonight is rose-gold and orchid. Narrow strata of clouds stretch across the west, pure gold. As I sit here, I just read Psalms 56 and 57. "For thy mercy is great unto the heavens, and thy truth unto the clouds. Be thou exalted, O God, above the heavens: let thy glory be above all the earth."

Such mercy amazes me. Sorry that I do not more ardently cast myself into the will of God . . . Today the thought occurred to me, Suppose He should ask me to wait five years? It stuns me to think of it. Yet—could I imagine that the mercy of God which has stretched to me from everlasting to everlasting could be exhausted in five years?

It's when one is living in the midst of those five years, or whatever the span may be, that it is easy to read spiritual books as nothing more than spiritual books, with no relation to the hard realities we are trying to cope with. Yet the deep principle of life out of death, so wonderfully illuminated for me by Lilias Trotter in her *Parables of the Cross,* has everything to do with the hard realities. There was real comfort for me in the lessons shown at the top of the stadium by the rainbow, the cloud, the words about the corn of wheat, the sunset. God spoke peace into my emotional turmoil because I was asking for it and looking for it and being silent enough to hear it.

To those with ears to hear and eyes to see, there will be very great release from unbearable burdens in the language of autumn trees, for example, when they dress most gloriously in preparation for death. The red of the leaves is the sign of the cross. Winter follows, when snow closes everything in frozen silence. The trees then are skeletons, but wonders are being performed under the surface of things. Spring comes, and the hidden wonders burst out all at once—tiny shoots, swelling buds, touches of green and red where all seemed hopeless the day before. Miss Trotter shows the yellow blossom of the gorse springing straight out of last year's thorn. Plain lessons for us, if we'll open our eyes.

If the leaves had not been let go to fall and wither, if the tree had not consented to be a skeleton for many months, there would be no new life rising, no bud, no flower, no fruit, no seed, no new generation.

I wonder what the flower and fruit have been in the life of another of my correspondents. She was in "winter" when she wrote about "this marvelous man" who had walked into her life, given her every reason to believe he was crazy about her, then drifted off into someone else's life. He had the *chutzpah* to come back from time to time to tell her how his new girlfriend was "filling voids" in his life which no one else had ever filled. *(What rubbish, I thought. What ails a man who would do such a thing? What ails the woman who will listen?)* The letter told me she had tried everything—dating others, being mad as a hornet, dwelling on his faults. She even thought of becoming a hermit. Nothing worked. She still wanted to be part of his life.

Was it all for nothing? The last part of the letter showed signs of spring:

> The Lord has brought about growth in me through knowing him, something I cannot regret, though there have been times when I wished I'd never met him. I have to give him to the Lord regularly. I live "present tense"

more than ever before and have managed to overcome the plaguing desire to know if "we" will eventually "work out." I've told the Lord I want to be an obedient servant, and He shot back, "And are you willing to face grief and pain or whatever it takes for Me to make you that?" Even though I felt unable, I said, "What choice do I have? I know too much to drop the ball now. There's no turning back." I'd be lying if I said I wasn't afraid. But He has brought me this far and already my joy is unspeakable.

17

What to Do
With Loneliness

Two lovers who are separated geographically can dwell
mentally in the past and the future, reliving the happiness
of having been together and anticipating the joy of
reunion. It is quite possible to waste the present altogether.
A letter from a schoolteacher shows that she did not mean
to waste it. She wanted to learn from the experience of
separation and loneliness.

We've been apart for six months, and we'll have five
days together at Easter when he's coming here. After that
he's off again for another eight months.

Paul takes things step by step and lives very much from
one day to the next. He's taught me a lot. I like to plan
ahead and know exactly where and when I'm going, even
when the Lord has wanted me to wait on Him.

Anyway, I've been reading Jim's journal and learning
a lot from what he went through during your long peri-

ods of separation. It's very much from a man's point of view, of course, and I want to know what went through your head then?

Sometimes this loneliness inside hurts so badly. It's not that no one loves me; I have wonderful parents and loving brothers and sisters. But I've experienced a loneliness this year like I've never had before, and I know a lot of it is due to the fact that I'm out of college and on my own for the first time.

How can I best handle this time?

Along with my reply I sent her a little leaflet I had written called *Loneliness*. This is what it says:

Be still and know that He is God. When you are lonely, too much stillness is exactly the thing that seems to be laying waste your soul. Use that stillness to quiet your heart before God. Get to know Him. If He is God, He is still in charge.

Remember that you are not alone. "The Lord, He it is that doth go with thee. He will not fail thee neither forsake thee. Be strong and of good courage." (Deut. 31:8) Jesus promised His disciples, "Lo, I am with you always." (Matt. 28:20) Never mind if you cannot feel His presence. He is there, never for one moment forgetting you.

Give thanks. In times of my greatest loneliness I have been lifted up by the promise of 2 Corinthians 4:17, 18, "For this slight momentary affliction is preparing for us an eternal weight of glory beyond all comparison, because we look not to the things that are seen but to the things that are unseen." This is something to thank God for. This loneliness itself, which seems a weight, will be far outweighed by glory.

Refuse self-pity. Refuse it absolutely. It is a deadly thing with power to destroy you. Turn your thoughts to Christ who has already carried your griefs and sorrows.

Accept your loneliness. It is one stage, and only one stage, on a journey that brings you to God. It will not always last.

Offer up your loneliness to God, as the little boy offered to
Jesus his five loaves and two fishes. God can transform it
for the good of others.

Do something for somebody else. No matter who or where you
are, there is something you can do, somebody who needs
you. Pray that you may be an instrument of God's peace,
that where there is loneliness you may bring joy.

The important thing is to receive this moment's experience with both hands. Don't waste it. "Wherever you
are, be all there," Jim once wrote. "Live to the hilt every
situation you believe to be the will of God."

A lovely moonlit night, but I am alone. Shall I resent
the very moonlight itself because my lover is somewhere
else?

A cozy candlelit supper with friends—couples, except
for me. Shall I be miserable all evening because they are
together and I am single? Have I been "cheated"? Who
cheated me?

The phone rings. Oh! Maybe it will be he! It's somebody
selling light bulbs. Shall I be rude because he ought to have
been somebody else?

A letter in the mailbox that (for once) doesn't look like
junk mail or a bill. I snatch it eagerly. It's from Aunt Susie.
Do I throw it aside in disgust?

I know all about this kind of response. I've been there
many times. Something I wrote to Jim once must have
revealed my resentment, for he wrote, "Let not our longing slay the appetite of our living." That was exactly what
I had let it do.

There were times, I'm sure, when if anyone had tried
to talk to me of the happiness of heaven I would have
turned away in a huff. The painful thing was that other
folks had not only heaven to look forward to, but they had
"all this and heaven, too," "this" being engagement or marriage. I was covetous. When the Apostle Paul wrote to the

Roman Christians about the happy certainty of heaven, he went on to say, "This doesn't mean, of course, that we have only a hope of future joys—we can be full of joy here and now even in our trials and troubles."

Even when I'm feeling most alone—on that moonlit night, in the middle of the candlelit supper, when the phone call and the letter don't come—can I be "full of joy, here and now"? Yes. That is what the Bible says. That means it must be not only true, but possible, and possible for me.

"Taken in the right spirit these very things will give us patient endurance; this in turn will develop a mature character, and a character of this sort produces a steady hope, a hope that will never disappoint us."

Taken in the right spirit. These are the operative words. The empty chair, the empty mailbox, the wrong voice on the phone have no particular magic in themselves that will make a mature character out of a lonely man or woman. They will never produce a steady hope. Not at all. The effect of my troubles depends not on the nature of the troubles themselves but on how I receive them. I can receive them with both hands in faith and acceptance, or I can rebel and reject. What they produce if I rebel and reject will be something very different from a mature character, something nobody is going to like.

Look at the choices:

rebellion—if this is the will of God for me now, He doesn't love me.

rejection—if this is what God is giving me, I won't have any part of it.

faith—God knows exactly what He's doing.

acceptance—He loves me; He plans good things for me; I'll take it.

The words "full of joy here and now" depend on the words "taken in the right spirit." You can't have one without the other. Taken in a spirit of trust, even loneliness contributes to the maturing of character, even the endurance of separation and silence and that hardest thing of all, uncertainty, can build in us a steady hope.

18

What Providence Has Gone and Done

In 1887 Mark Twain was in New York, waiting for his wife, Livy, to come from Hartford to attend a dinner with him and then go to spend a week in Washington. A blizzard prevented her. Twain wrote:

And so, after all my labor and persuasion to get you to at last promise to take a week's holiday and go off with me on a lark, this is what Providence has gone and done about it. A mere simple *request* to you to stay at home would have been entirely sufficient: but no, that is not big enough, picturesque enough—a blizzard's the idea: pour down all the snow in stock, turn loose all the winds, bring a whole continent to a stand-still: that is Providence's idea of the correct way to trump a person's trick. Dear me, if I had known it was going to make all this trouble and cost all these millions, I never would have said anything *about* your going to Washington.

The hundreds of pages of journals and diaries which describe my own agonies of soul would convince even the most cynical reader that the writer was not *reluctant* to do what God wanted her to do. Often confused, occasionally fearful, sometimes pitiful or fanatical or misguided, but seldom reluctant. Nearly always, I should think, determined to obey. Wouldn't a mere simple request from God to trust Him be sufficient? Is it absolutely necessary for Him to yank out of sight whatever we most prize, to drag us into spiritual traumas of the severest sort, to strip us naked in the winds of His purifying Spirit in order that we should learn to trust?

But I am overreacting. I am dramatizing the commonest experience. What are these silly matters of the heart, compared to real tribulation? Talk about lessons in trust. Have a look at what the Apostle Paul suffered: shipwrecks, flogging, public lashings, imprisonment, chains, stocks, starvation, nakedness—and all this heaped on a man who, in spite of years of having persecuted Christians, had been transformed in an instant into God's faithful servant. It does seem, as Mark Twain said, "the oddest thing—the way Providence manages." Saint Theresa expressed a similar perplexity: "If this is the way You treat Your friends, no wonder You have so few."

But hear Paul's testimony of trust:

> Who can separate us from the love of Christ? Can trouble, pain or persecution? Can lack of clothes or food, danger to life and limb, the threat of force of arms? Indeed some of us know the truth of that ancient text:
> For Thy sake we are killed all the day long;
> We were accounted as sheep for the slaughter.
> No, in all these things we win an overwhelming victory through him who has proved his love for us.
> I have become absolutely convinced that neither death nor life, neither messenger of Heaven nor monarch of

earth, neither what happens today nor what may happen tomorrow, neither a power from on high nor a power from below, nor anything else in God's whole world has any power to separate us from the love of God in Christ Jesus our Lord!

A remarkable statement of what faith is about. "Killed all the day long"—yet a winner. Trouble, pain, persecution, and all the rest—but "overwhelming victory." Now this is the amazing thing: The victory is not escape or exemption or protection from any of the things listed. Paul went through them. He did not escape trouble. He was not exempt from human woes. God did not protect even this Very Important Person from public floggings or starvation or anything else. Yet Paul was able to say he was winning the victory through Him who has proved His love for us. How? How had He proved His love?

Our vision is so limited we can hardly imagine a love that does not show itself in protection from suffering. The love of God is of a different nature altogether. It does not hate tragedy. It never denies reality. It stands in the very teeth of suffering. The love of God did not protect His own Son. That was the proof of His love—that He gave that Son, that He let Him go to Calvary's cross, though "legions of angels" might have rescued Him. He will not necessarily protect us—not from anything it takes to make us like His Son. A lot of hammering and chiseling and purifying by fire will have to go into the process.

Look at the last paragraph of Paul's ringing manifesto: *"I have become absolutely convinced* that nothing in God's whole world has any power to separate me from the love of God in Christ Jesus my Lord."

"Nothing, Paul? What about death?"

"No, not death."

"Life?"

"No, not life."

"Messenger of Heaven?"

"No messenger of Heaven can do it."

"Monarch of earth?"

"Not even a monarch of earth."

"What happens today?"

"Nope."

"Tomorrow?"

"Nope."

"A power from on high?"

"No power from on high."

"From below?"

"No power from below."

"Anything else in God's whole world?"

"Nothing else whatsoever. Absolutely nothing."

"Paul, I think you forgot something."

"Did I?"

"Love life. Matters of the heart. I'll take the floggings and the shipwrecks and the persecution—those are things people are supposed to bear for Christ. But what if the woman I love turns me down? What if the man I've got my eye on doesn't even look at me? What if I'm rejected? What if . . ."

"Oh. I never thought of that."

Is that the answer you'd expect the apostle to give? He'd forgotten all about love's terrors and pitfalls. If he'd thought of them, he would not have been able to say "in all *these* things we win an overwhelming victory." He wouldn't have said "nor anything else in God's whole world" would he? He'd have had to say "nor anything else except my passions, my poor broken heart, my miserable bad luck in my love life, has any power to separate me from the love of God." He'd have added that God can take care of the big things—Paul had plenty of proof of that.

Perhaps matters of the heart would seem like little things to Paul. I have a hunch they would. Well then—

what about those? Can *they* put us beyond His love and redemption?

The point is that we have to learn to trust in little things, even in what may seem like silly things, if we are ever going to be privileged to suffer in the big things. "The man who can be trusted in little things can be trusted also in great; and the man who is dishonest in little things is dishonest also in great things. If, then, you have not proved trustworthy with the wealth of this world, who will trust you with the wealth that is real?"

Years after the end of the Jim Elliot story, my mother said something to me about my "suffering" during those waiting years. It came as a surprise to me, for though I would never have denied that the trail was a bit rugged, I had not thought of it as suffering. Shipwrecks, floggings, physical pain, yes, those I would call suffering, but not my aching heart. However, it's no use trying to measure suffering. What matters is making the right use of it, taking advantage of the sense of helplessness it brings to turn one's thoughts to God. Trust is the lesson. Jesus loves me, this I know—not because He does just what I'd like, but because the Bible tells me so. Calvary proves it. He loved me and gave Himself for me.

19

The Rebel Sigh

As I was writing in the journal I knew that the picture I was painting was far from complete. How could it be complete? I could not see it whole myself. Only God could do that. And if I could have, how could I put it all into words? That word *ashes* came to mind often, the word we had used that evening under the stone cross—a word for nothingness, the aching void.

> *July 6—The emptiness turns me again to Him. I remember the old hymn,*
>
> > *Teach me to feel that Thou art always nigh;*
> > *Teach me the struggles of the soul to bear—*
> > *To check the rising doubt, the rebel sigh;*
> > *Teach me the patience of unanswered prayer.*
> >
> > George Croly
> > *"Spirit of God, Descend upon My Heart"*

Does the fact that I do not forget Jim indicate that God does not want me to, or is it my own unwillingness to forget that has kept God from answering my prayer to that end? Or does He want me to remember—to "suffer me to hunger" so that I might the more fully learn to find all my satisfaction in Him? . . . Can it be that by a show of what Paul calls "will worship" I should crush the bud of a flower of God's creation? I know no prayer other than Thy will be done.

The hope was always there that God's will would bring us together. It might not be that, I knew, and I realized that the deepest spiritual lessons are not learned by His letting us have our way in the end, but by His making us wait, bearing with us in love and patience until we are able honestly to pray what He taught His disciples to pray: Thy will be done. Acceptance of whatever that means is the great victory of faith that overcomes the world. The diary records a prayer asking to be led higher. Was this the answer to that? If so, I needed more grace, for heart and flesh were feeble.

"Commit thy way unto the Lord; . . . and he shall bring it to pass." Sometimes I was sure "it" would mean marriage. Other times I had to accept it to mean the will of God, which could be anything, including, of course, permanent virginity. I found that the commitment had to be reaffirmed almost daily. It was the taking up of the cross daily that Jesus spoke of. Is it a tough thing to do? Then do it. Take it up at once. Say yes to God. He will bring the very best to pass.

Is it dishonest to say yes to God when you don't really feel like it? Is it lying to Him to say "I'll do Your will" when your heart tells you you really want something else? You recognize that "rebel sigh" that the hymn writer mentions.

Those questions often troubled me. Now I see it this way. If you love someone, there are many things you will do for that person because *you love him*—not because it's what

89

you'd prefer if love did not enter the picture. The fact is, love has entered the picture. Therefore, in your heart, you can be very honest when you tell him you really *prefer* to do what He wants, because, more than your own pleasure, you want His. When obedience to God contradicts what I think will give me pleasure, let me ask myself if I love Him. If I can say yes to that question, can't I say yes to pleasing Him? Can't I say yes even if it means a sacrifice? A little quiet reflection will remind me that yes to God *always* leads in the end to joy. We can absolutely bank on that.

Another great comfort to me during the long uncertainty was the knowledge that I was being prayed for, not only by friends and family, but—wonder of wonders—by Christ Himself, who always lives to intercede for us, and by the Holy Spirit, who ". . . comes to the aid of our weakness. We do not even know how we ought to pray, but through our inarticulate groans the Spirit himself is pleading for us, and God who searches our inmost being knows what the Spirit means, because He pleads for God's people in God's own way."

It would be the easy road if the desire itself simply disappeared. That thought recurred in my journal and was expressed in a letter from a young woman recently:

> I met a young man in the spring and over the summer acquired quite an affection for him. I felt he was the man I could marry. I remember after our first date kneeling beside my bed thanking the Lord for this man and asking if I could be his wife . . . . He had difficulty discerning where I fitted in, told me I aroused certain desires in him, but felt immature, thought it was best to curtail our friendship. He has been overseas for a year now, but I continue to yearn for him. I continually ask the Lord to take away this desire to be with him and share my life with him. This affection is terribly painful. Though I am busy with studies and my work, I still ache in my heart. I am struggling so. Of all the

people I know, it is you I feel can truly empathize with my present situation.

Bless her heart. I can, but I don't know why she thought so. I wonder if she allowed the man to see her eagerness and scared him? Possibly her failure to wait quietly caused him to "curtail the friendship." The last part of my diary entry of that same evening when I pondered the rainbow in the stadium says:

> *The flesh looks at the smooth road and thinks it would be easier if I were made to forget completely, or were given an answer soon. Psalm 57: "... In the shadow of thy wings will I make my refuge, until these calamities be overpast. ... God that performeth all things for me ... My heart is fixed: I will sing and give praise."*

If the yearnings went away, what would we have to offer up to the Lord? Aren't they given to us to offer? It is the control of passion, not its eradication, that is needed. How would we learn to submit to the authority of Christ if we had nothing to submit?

My little niece Gallaudet Howard taught me something important when she was about three years old. Seeing that she was having difficulty with the sleeves, I asked her if I could help her put her dress on. "Oh, never mind," she said. "Papa usually lets me struggle." What kind of a father is that? A wise one. Her father, my brother Tom, is also a very sensitive one, aware of the importance of struggle in the process of growth.

I found in my Greek New Testament that 1 Peter 5:10 could be translated, "After you have suffered a while, he himself will mend that which was broken." If all struggles and sufferings were eliminated, the spirit would no more reach maturity than would the child. The Heavenly Father wants to see us grow up.

20

Self-deception

The old English word denoting that part of us which constantly wars against the spirit is *flesh*. Yet the story of Jesus' life reveals that He was a man, really a man, fully a man. He was a man of flesh in the ordinary physical sense. He ate, drank, walked, slept, became weary, sat down at a well to drink in the heat of the day. We know He was sinless, so we must conclude that there was absolutely nothing inherently sinful in the physical stuff of which His body was made—the bone, muscle, tissue, blood. There is nothing sinful in our bone, muscle, tissue, or blood either.

What is it then that is at war with the spiritual life? Can we be human and holy at the same time? This question came to the fore in my lucubrations about Jim. My love for him was human. I wanted it also to be—I hoped and prayed that it would be—holy.

There is room for self-deception here. A girl wrote, "I am twenty-one years old and sister/friend with a twenty-three-year-old man. We both want to seek God more seriously and consistently. I have never before been involved with a guy whose greatest desire for our relationship is to love me only purely and build me up in the Lord. I greatly appreciate his attitude, but I'm not graceful in responding and much of this is brand-new to me, although the most wonderful and healing relationship I've ever had."

The bewilderment comes when you mix up words like *involved* and *relationship* with the idea of loving "only purely," for the purpose of "building up in the Lord." It is possible to deny the strongest human drive, sexuality, and to spiritualize what is a thoroughly natural and human hunger for marriage. The girl does not know what to call this relationship except sister/friend. Surely she was much more interested in this man than she was in any other man to whom she was a sister or a friend. Every man of her acquaintance, I suppose, would fall into one or the other of those categories. But this particular twenty-three-year-old occupied her attention. His greatest desire, she tells me, was to love her "only purely." Bravo. If by that he meant to love her as any Christian is to love any other Christian, as a member of the Body of Christ, then why does she use the word *involved?* She is involved with this guy, she has the "most wonderful and healing relationship" she's ever had. He sounds pretty special to me. It has the earmarks not of sister/brother or friend/friend but of lover/beloved. She doesn't know, probably, if she's beloved or not, and she's not admitting, to me at any rate, that she loves him. But her feelings are—what else?—sexual.

Paul was a very earthy man. He did not deceive himself about the power of women over men or vice versa. He knew the drives, was acquainted with the pitfalls, and very sensibly told the Christians of Corinth ". . . it is good for a man not to touch a woman." ". . . It is a good thing for a man to have nothing to do with women; but because there is so much immorality, let each man have his own wife and each woman her own husband." In other words, when you get to the point where you can't keep your hands off each other, it's time to get married. The current "touchy-poo" brand of Christianity had no place in Paul's thinking. He never said, "Let each man have his own relationship."

My father counseled his four sons never to say "I love you" to a woman until they were ready to follow immediately with "Will you marry me?" Nor should they think of saying "Will you marry me?" unless they had first said "I love you." How much pain and confusion would be averted if men followed that rule.

Jim didn't follow it, of course. He told me he loved me. He did not ask me to marry him. I was thrilled, overwhelmed, devastated. *Better to know I'm loved than not to know at all* was my thought. One can pine alone, but the knowledge that love is reciprocated enormously increases the longing for fulfillment.

Can I recommend Jim's plan of action to others? Never in a million years. I feel quite certain he would not have wanted anyone to build a doctrine on it. But the situation was unusual. Not that he was called to a lifetime of celibacy. He did not know whether it was for life. He did not need to know. He was called to stay single, unattached, uncommitted at least until he had had missionary experience. He had reason to believe that he had awakened love in a dedicated woman and that he could trust her with the information he wanted to give her. It was a risk. He knew that, and he took it. I didn't go and jump off a bridge. God kept us. But I scratched my head and wrung my hands over the question of human versus holy. Was it possible to love him as intensely as I did and to be pure enough to desire nothing more in the world than his holiness and happiness? I can only say that I tried. "What hindereth thee more than thine affections not fully mortified to the will of God?" wrote Thomas à Kempis in *Imitation of Christ.*

Mortified. A frightening word. If my affections must be mortified, does that mean they must be killed? Does it mean they're all evil and sinful and wicked? Is it wicked to love a man or a woman in any way other than as a sister or brother or friend?

There is no getting around the etymology of the word *mortify.* It comes from the Latin for *death.* The King James Version of Romans 8:13 says we must mortify our members. A modern translation makes it even more direct. "But if by the Spirit you *put to death* all the base pursuits of the body, then you will live." What are base pursuits? There is a list in Colossians 3:5: fornication, indecency, lust, foul cravings, and the ruthless greed which is nothing less than idolatry. These are the *products* of human desire, if human desire is given free rein. The Christian has handed the reins over to his Master. His human desires are brought into line. The desires still exist, are still strong, natural, and human, but they are subjugated to the higher power of the Spirit. They are purified and corrected as we live day by day in faith and obedience.

For the outlook of the lower nature is enmity with God; it is not subject to the law of God; indeed it cannot be: those who live on such a level cannot possibly please God.

But that is not how you live. You are on the spiritual level, if only God's Spirit dwells within you; and if a man does not possess the Spirit of Christ, he is no Christian. But if Christ is dwelling within you, then although the body is a dead thing because you sinned, yet the spirit is life itself because you have been justified. Moreover, if the Spirit of him who raised Jesus from the dead dwells within you, then the God who raised Christ Jesus from the dead will also give new life to your mortal bodies through his indwelling Spirit.

It follows, my friends, that our lower nature has no claim upon us; we are not obliged to live on that level.

95

That spells it out. Two natures, lower and higher, flesh and spirit. The lower one has no claim on us. The nonbeliever denies this, listens to the promptings of the flesh, capitulates, insists he has to do what feels good, to go with the flow. The Christian mortifies the flesh by submitting to the authority of Christ—to His authority in every area of his being, including his God-given but very dangerous sexuality. It's dangerous as dynamite. Fire and water, too, are gifts of God, but when they get out of control, the result is devastation.

The letter quoted earlier in this chapter is one of many like it which I have received. There is confusion about relationships. There is an unwillingness to come straight out and say "I'm nuts about this girl; I've got to have her." In other words, sexual desire is camouflaged in spiritual terms. What one knows is far from platonic—is, in fact, plainly erotic—is called a friendship, a relationship, an involvement, an experience.

Another girl wrote:

A young man whom I met at a party last year and for whom I cared profoundly *vanished* last November. Since then I have been bitter at God. Bitterness and anger toward God has caused my I-don't-care attitude toward many people around me, even people at church.

The dreaming, 'inspirational right half" of my brain tells me I will never really be fulfilled, sexually or otherwise, unless I'm married. How can I overcome my bitterness toward God? How can I overcome my insatiable desire to know *why* God acts as He does, rather than just trusting Him? Will God *ever* tell me how that young man is getting along in life? Will I *ever* know if he is a Christian?

There is honesty there—she knows she is bitter toward God. There's the crux of her sin. There is self-deception also. It doesn't really matter whether the man is getting along in life. He may be president of Exxon. So what? It doesn't matter if he's a Christian, actually. What matters is is he coming back? Does the girl really want to know why God acts as He does (the Bible is full of clues), or does she want Him to quit acting that way? She's furious at Him because the man doesn't love her, never did love her, probably never will.

Let's be candid with ourselves before God. Call a spade a spade or even a muddy shovel. If your passions are aroused, say so—to yourself and to God, *not* to the object of your passion. Then turn the reins over to God. Bring your will to Him. Will to obey Him, ask for His help. He will not do the obeying for you, but He will help you. Don't ask me how. He knows how. You'll see.

21

What Women Do to Men

Women are always tempted to be initiators. We like to get things done. We want to talk about situations and feelings, get it all out in the open, deal with it. It appears to us that men often ignore and evade issues, sweep things under the rug, forget about them, get on with projects, business, pleasures, sports, eat a big steak, turn on the television, roll over, and go to sleep. Women respond to this tendency by insisting on confrontation, communication, showdown. If we can't dragoon our men into that, we nag, we plead, we get attention by tears, silence, or withholding warmth and intimacy. We have a large bag of tricks.

C. S. Lewis's vision of purgatory was a place where milk was always boiling over, crockery smashing, and toast burning. The lesson assigned to the men was to do something about it. The lesson for the women was to do nothing. That would be purgatory for most of us. Women, especially when it comes to the love life, can hardly stand to do nothing.

A young woman came to me after a meeting to tell me she was going to be a missionary. "Good!" I said.

"And I'm going to get married."

"Wonderful. When?"

"Well, I don't know when exactly. You see, I'm not engaged or anything."

"But you're getting married?"

"The Lord has told me I am."

"Has He told you who the man is?"

"Oh yes, he goes to this church, we're good friends and—"

"Whatever you do, don't tell him what the Lord has told you."

"But I already have. I called him right away. He wasn't sure about it, I mean, you know, like, he hadn't really felt called to the mission field or anything, you know; he was, like, surprised, but—"

"You'd better leave him alone until the Lord tells *him* something."

"I can't do that, I mean—what if he doesn't understand that this is the Lord's will? I try to call him every few days to remind him. He seems sorta cool, you know, but he's thinking about it, I'm sure. Like, you know, he's really my friend and all, but, well, I just know God is going to work it out."

That man had my sympathies.

Another woman wrote:

I've had nearly six months to digest your speech on submission, and now I'm seeking your advice. The matter concerns a young man I became very attached to. I committed the matter to the Lord in prayer. I eventually dealt with the situation by writing to him and tactfully making my feelings known. He did not reciprocate my affection, but assured me that he wanted to continue our friendship. I have written him three other letters in three months. None of these have been answered. I called him, mostly to make sure I could still talk to him. Two months later I called again, mainly to assure myself that he was still alive. He was rather cool.

In none of my letters or calls have I attempted to push myself on him. I wanted to return to our status as friends as he suggested we do.

I no longer understand him.

Poor girl. She had no business in the first place "tactfully" making her feelings known. Poor choice of words. A woman taking that kind of initiative is not tactful. Very likely she scuttled any chances she might have had with the man. When he did not reply, she had a clear signal that he was not interested. To continue to try to arouse his interest by writing and calling was worse than useless.

I can imagine his thoughts when he picked up the phone and heard her voice. *Oh, no, not her again. What the heck do I do now?* She's sweet, cheerful, friendly, maybe a little breathless. *How can I get her off my back?* The only course open to him was to be, as she said, rather cool. Any other response she would have taken as encouragement.

She called again. This time, perhaps, not quite so cheerful. Maybe she breathed heavily, spoke plaintively. I'm only guessing. She did not attempt to push herself, she said. Hadn't she? She was unfair to him and dishonest with herself, only wanted to assure herself he was alive. There are other ways of ascertaining that. In truth she was crying, "I'm here. Please love me."

She said she did not understand him. I did. He didn't love her. I tried to explain this. If he had loved her, he would have pursued her. He did not want to hurt her, but she would not let go.

A letter published in a Christian magazine's advice column says, "I have been a widow for more than twenty years and thought I was over my sorrow and my romantic notions. Recently I met a man my age who had lost his wife. When I expressed sympathy, he seemed very appreciative and began to pay quite a bit of attention to me. The long and the short of it is that I fell in love with him." So far so good. Women do that. The letter goes on, "Then the conference ended, and I went home. There was a phone call or two from him, then nothing. Next thing I knew he was dating another person." Men do that, too. The amazing part to me was the columnist's reply: "If this man is as fickle as he seems to be, you can be glad that the relationship is over now, rather than later. It would be a far greater heartache to live the rest of your life with someone you could not trust."

Fickle? Someone you could not trust? What was the columnist talking about? It was the lady who first expressed sympathy. The man was glad to get that. He paid attention to her, but it was only a conference. How many days were there in which to build a relationship? The lady doesn't say he had told her he was in love with her. He made a phone call or two. That was nice of him. What else was he supposed to do?

Her expectations were entirely unreasonable. I would like to ask her what she would have said if somebody at the conference had remarked, "Well! You seem to have a thing going with that widower!" I suspect she would have retorted, "How ridiculous! His wife just died! Can't two people even sit together without everybody's assuming they're in love?" Yet here she is now expecting much more of the poor man, resenting his dating somebody else. She's been treated shabbily, the columnist tells her.

I protest. Women expect too much of men.

I can hear the howls of protest from the women. "Men want to play around. They lead us on, try to get what they can out of us, deceive us," and so on. True enough. Which is exactly why I beg women to wait. Wait on God. Keep your mouth shut. Don't expect anything until the declaration is clear and forthright.

And to the men I say be careful with us, please. Be circumspect.

Before Jim went to Ecuador, a young woman made it quite obvious to him, and especially to the women in their church, that she was interested in him. She had announced that God had called her to the mission field, but she was not certain as to which field until Jim declared he was going to Ecuador. Ah. That was it. Ecuador was where God wanted her, too, she said. Always wanting to act in truth and help others to do the same, Jim asked the girl to lunch. He wasted little time in small talk, but put it quite plainly that if she had any feelings for him they were misdirected. He told her he had made up his mind as to whom he would marry if God ever showed him that He wanted him to marry.

A woman ought to be as honest with a man who shows an interest in her. A few months before my engagement to my second husband was made public, a widower whom I had known slightly in college came to visit me. It was a long journey by car, and he brought his daughters with him. We went out to dinner and he put his "cards on the table"—told me he was testing the prospect of marriage. I thanked him and put mine on the table. "I'm not sure I'll ever remarry," I said, "but if I do, I'm pretty sure I know who it will be." He sent me a bouquet of roses with a card, "With affectionate jealousy."

A good-looking nephew of mine is often asked out by women. "Sorry," he tells them. "That isn't the way I do it. When I go out with a lady, I like to do the asking. But thanks anyway."

Resist the temptation to trifle with other people's feelings. It may be fun to "play the fish," like a trout on a fly line, but it is cruel, it is dishonest, and it is dangerous.

22

What Do Men Look For?

My mother was Spoon Girl of the class of 1917 at Germantown Friends School in Philadelphia when Leonard Carmichael (later president of the Smithsonian Institution) was Cane Man. As best all-around girl and boy of the graduating class, they received engraved awards: she a large silver spoon and he a silver-headed cane. Mother was slim, dark-haired, blue-eyed. She was one of the first women in the city to drive a car. Her father had given her a big Buick, and she cut quite a figure in her raccoon coat and beaver hat. She had an assortment of boyfriends. When I was growing up, she gave me two and only two pieces of advice on that subject: Let them do the chasing and keep them at arm's length.

But what if they don't chase? What if they never get within arm's length?

Here are four stories told me on this subject.

"I want to be married," said the first person, a college student. "I love this guy with all my heart. But he seems so casual about a relationship which to me is very deep. I hardly know how to pray about this."

The second, a young career woman, sat at my kitchen table one morning and said, "He didn't speak to me for days. We had a really great thing going. I mean, he was calling every night, taking me out two or three times a week, sending me flowers. All of a sudden, nothing. So I bump into him in the elevator, in the hall, different places—he works in the same building—and what does he do? Turns the other way. 'Come *on*,' I finally said, 'Don't *ignore* me!' You know—does that make sense, just to ignore me? I mean, couldn't we at least *discuss* it?"

Maybe you could, if he wants to. But if he doesn't want to, what do you gain by collaring him and saying "Talk to me!"?

The third person wrote me a letter. "Is it all right as a female to ask a male friend out, or is that considered chasing a person? I have done that a few times with a neat Christian friend, but he has paid for something. Plus, I do not consider myself chasing him."

The fourth: "He was a very positive and joyous young man who makes you feel like you're the only person who is important to him as you talk. I fell for him, though I had prayed that God would guard my heart with all diligence. We had a wonderful time at the student conference, and one cold but clear evening we went for a long walk all over campus and had pizza by the fire. He also went to hear you speak at one session and couldn't stop talking about what you said, especially the part about men initiating and women responding. Needless to say, since I've returned home I've sat here waiting to respond—if he would initiate, by writing or calling. He hasn't done either."

Four women in the same boat. Attracted to men who aren't attracted to them—at least not enough to do anything about it. What to do? One prays, but is not sure how to pray. The second confronts. The third asks for a date, but lets him pay for part of it. The fourth waits. For all I know, not one of them got what she really wanted.

In this day of liberation and equality and role options, should we bother about who does what? I don't even know what to call it. *Wooing* may be a little archaic. *Courting? Chasing? Hunting? Pursuing?*

"Just do what feels good, never mind the vocabulary," someone will suggest.

Easier said than done. I find that people aren't nearly as sure as they thought they'd be about what feels good. Maybe there's something more deeply awry than a silly rule about who makes the phone call.

One evening last winter my husband and I invited a group of single men from a theological seminary to sit around our fireplace and talk about what single Christian men expect of single Christian women. We hear a great deal from the women on this subject, and on what they expect of men, but we had not heard much from the men. We were not asking what they were looking for, first of all, in a wife, but simply what they expect in ordinary, everyday social contact.

"Do you want women to do the asking?" was one of my questions.

"It's a shock," somebody said.

"A turnoff," somebody else said.

"If a woman is smart, she knows the best place for her to be, according to Scripture, is submission. A man is supposed to serve because he is the head," one man said.

"Submission is a command to married women, isn't it?" I said. "What do you expect in ordinary give-and-take on campus?"

"Total honesty."

"Oh. Hmm. Total honesty. Then suppose she comes to you in the hall one day," I suggested, "and says, 'I think you're the handsomest stud on the Hill. I've been dreaming about you every night for three weeks. The Lord has told me we should establish a caring and sharing relationship.' She's honest (maybe). Is that what you're asking for?"

"Oh, heck no. I didn't mean that."

"What, then?"

Long silence. Head scratching. Then the answers began to come.

Femininity.

Affirmation.

Encouragement.

Tenderness.

Sensitivity.

Vulnerability.

"She need not be gorgeous, though I wouldn't hold that against her!"

"I'd like a woman to present some kind of challenge. If there's caution on her part, that interests me."

"Edginess about marriage is easy to spot."

"Yeah. I look for women who are secure in the Lord. Content. Can handle adversity."

"Quietly courageous."

"Not trying to please everybody. But free to pay a compliment now and then, if it's an honest one."

"Maternal. That's important. Women should be maternal."

I was glad we had invited no women that evening. They would have had a hard time keeping their mouths shut.

There was one thing we did not talk about, so far as I recall. It is mystery. A man likes to think there is more in a woman than he can fathom. How much is there that only God knows about? Years after I was in Bible school, a man told me he used to sit in class and stare at me, wondering what in the world was going through my head. Something signaled a mystery there, he said, and it fascinated him. The message we were receiving as the seminary men talked around our fireplace was that they did not want to be told everything the women were thinking. They wanted to be left to wonder about it and to find out for themselves.

A woman's beauty should reside, according to the Apostle Peter, in the inmost center of her being, an ". . . imperishable ornament, a gentle, quiet spirit, which is of high value in the sight of God."

23

The Mess We've Made

Nora Ephron, in her novel *Heartburn,* says that the major achievement of the 1970s is the Dutch treat. Is that what men and women want?

I have the feeling the world's not going around very smoothly anymore. There's been a breakdown somewhere when men sit around waiting for the phone to ring and women get angry if a man holds a door open for them.

The conduct of men and women in every society on earth up till now has always been seen as a fairly delicate and potentially explosive business. For that reason it has been surrounded with customs, taboos, rituals, prohibitions, protocol, courtesies. Have we been wise to discard them?

Five centuries before Christ, Euripides compared male and female to heaven and earth. "It is love which causes Earth to yearn for rain, when the parched ground, barren with drought, has need of moisture. It is Love which makes the Sacred Heaven, swollen with rain, sink into the lap of

Earth. And when these twain are mingled, they beget and nourish all things."

We crave order, design, harmony. The way we live and behave ought to have some congruence with the fundamental order of the universe. Is it significant at all, we may ask, that it has, until very recently, seemed incongruous for women to lead and men to follow? Even in matrilineal societies the positions of highest prestige went to men, and as for "matriarchal" societies, it seems that they are legendary. Not a single one has been found. Stephen Goldberg says in *The Inevitability of Patriarchy:*

> I have consulted the original ethnographic materials on every society I have ever seen alleged by anyone to represent a matriarchy, female dominance, or the association of high-status, nonmaternal roles with women. . . . I have found no society that represents any of these. Furthermore, I believe that the evidence advanced in Chapter Three renders the concept of matriarchy and an absence of male dominance as absurd as the possibility that there was a society that associated childbirth with males. But it must be admitted that one cannot *prove* that matriarchy or anything else has never existed. If one wants to demonstrate that there has never been a centaur he can merely invoke the realities of physiology and evolution to indicate the biological improbability of a centaur's ever having existed and demonstrate that the evidence alleging the past existence of a centaur is worthless. If the reader insists on maintaining a belief in a once-existent matriarchal society all we can do is demand from him some evidence more convincing than his desire for there to have been one.

More and more biological evidence is turning up which indicates that many of the behavioral differences between the sexes are determined by hormones. This is rather upsetting to those who would prefer to believe they are determined by social conditioning. For Christians conduct must be governed not by the findings of sociologists, anthropologists, or biologists, interesting as those may be, rather ". . . in our dealings with our fellow-men . . . our conduct has been governed by a devout and godly sincerity, by the grace of God and not by worldly wisdom."

By the grace of God we have not been left to ourselves in the matter of who is to do the initiating. Adam needed a helper. God fashioned one to the specifications of his need and brought her to him. It was Adam's job to husband her, that is, he was responsible—to care for, protect, provide for, and cherish her. Males, as the physical design alone would show, are made to be initiators. Females are made to be receptors, responders. It was not arbitrarily that God called Himself Israel's bridegroom and Israel His Bride, nor Christ the Head and the Church the Body and the Bride. He woos us, calls us, wins us, gives us His name, shares with us His destiny, takes responsibility for us, loves us with a love stronger than death.

The spiritual paradigm defines the relationship of men and women, specifically of husbands and wives, since that is the central human union. The symbols matter enormously. They matter *enormously*, because they represent the relative positions of Christ and the Church.

Adam and Eve made a mess of things when they reversed roles. She took the initiative, offered him the forbidden fruit, and he, instead of standing as her protector, responded and sinned along with her. It's been chaos ever since. No wonder that the further we move from the original order the more confused we become. "A shock." "A turnoff." The responses of the seminary men are not, I believe, conditioned only by custom. Something else makes them feel in their bones that women are out of place when they become initiators in so fragile and subtle a matter as courtship.

There are signs of confusion far worse than women chasing men. Homosexuality, teenage pregnancy, divorce, abortion, the new "house-husband" role, new translations of the Bible to eliminate "sexist" language, women suing the New York fire department because they flunked the test for "firepersons"—signs that the congruous has become incongruous. The order disordered. The complementary competitive. The glory of our sexuality, in short, is tarnished.

"Look," a young woman says, "I'm not arguing theology and all that. All I'm thinking about is phoning Al to ask if he'd like to go out for some Chinese food. Anything wrong with that?"

That depends. Al might think it was a great idea. Joe might not. "Be careful," I say to the woman. "Don't put him in an indefinable position. Have you considered the paradigms and symbols? Does the word *modesty* ring any bells with you? Is *reserve* an outmoded word now? If you should marry Al in the end, would you (would he?) want to live with the knowledge that you went after him? He might resent you for snaring him. You might despise him for allowing you to."

"It was worth the risk," some will say. "We're both glad it worked out that way." I imagine they are the sort who will say that women have a right to go to war and no right to be protected in any way in which men are not protected. I prefer not to get into the ring with those who take that line of thought.

I would ask my challengers to reflect on the design of the Designer; to ask what it means; to test the way they treat the opposite sex with these questions: Is it fitting? Is it in accord with the pattern I'd like my life to follow? Does it harmonize with my best understanding of God's plan? What is it that brings God's man and God's woman near to each other with delicacy and grace? Do I want to walk, here as in all areas of my life, by faith, or will I take things into my own hands?

"Well, how 'bout if I just call and ask him what I can pray for for him this week?"

You have not yet understood.

24

Hot Sweats and Wet Feet

It costs Christ and all His followers sharp showers and hot sweats ere they win to the top of the mountain. But still our soft nature would have heaven coming to our bedside when we are sleeping, and lying down with us, that we might go to heaven in warm clothes; but all that came there found wet feet by the way, and sharp storms that did take the hide off their face, and found to's and fro's and up's and down's, and many enemies by the way.

Samuel Rutherford

It is always the quick answer, the simple solution, we look for, entirely forgetting that heaven doesn't come to our bedside. The violent, Jesus said, take it by force.

I tried to tell myself that it was not the waiting or the separation or the uncertainty that was hardest to take, but the silence.

August 17, 1948—Silence begins to drag on my soul. It is a kind of waiting which hears no voice, no footstep, sees no sign. I feel that I could wait ten years, if it were not this *waiting, this* silence. *I have spent the evening by a little pool which held the silent sky in its heart. There was no ripple, no stir.* Lord, let me *be that pool.*

That "dragging on the soul," that stretched-out agony of longing—what are these but the sharp showers, hot sweats, wet feet of which that old saint Rutherford wrote so often? His letters are full of them. There has never been any other route to glory. From the earliest stories of Israel to the story of His Son's journey as a man on earth, God has been bringing men always through much tribulation. There is no Strawberry Shortcut.

Was it necessary for God to test the fiber of His children for forty years in the wilderness? Wouldn't forty days have been enough? The process must go on . . . and on . . . and on.

John Buchan put it this way: "You have chosen the roughest road, but it goes straight to the hilltops."

Through affairs of the heart God uncovers our true intentions: ". . . whether or no it was in your heart to keep his commandments. He humbled you and made you hungry; then he fed you on manna. . . ."

But it was not manna the people wanted. It was leeks and onions and garlic. It was meat and bread, wine and oil—ordinary food.

So it is with us. We're created men and women. If Adam needed Eve and she was made for him, isn't it natural, then, isn't it altogether fitting and proper, that men and women should hunger for each other?

It is natural indeed. However, it's not the only thing God has in mind for us. We are not meant to live merely by what is natural. We need to learn to live by the supernatural. Ordinary fare will not fill the emptiness in our hearts. Bread will not suffice. We need extraordinary fare. We need manna. How else will we learn to eat it, if we are

113

never hungry? How will we educate our tastes for heavenly things if we are surfeited with earthly? Sex simply will not suffice any more than bread will.

My heart was saying, "Lord, take away this longing, or give me that for which I long." The Lord was answering, "I must teach you to long for something better."

". . . He fed you on manna which neither you nor your fathers had known before, to teach you that man cannot live on bread alone but lives by every word that comes from the mouth of the Lord."

God knew that giving me Jim when I wanted him would not provide the far more important training I needed for things to come. It was in learning to eat that Living Bread, sufficient always for one day at a time (not in advance for the five years I feared) that I was taught and disciplined and prepared for later things.

July 6—From Robert Louis Stevenson: "Anyone can carry his burden, however heavy, until nightfall. Anyone can do his work, however hard, for one day. Anyone can live sweetly, patiently, lovingly, purely, till the sun goes down. And this is all that life really means."

Take therefore no thought for the morrow. . . .
Give us this day our daily bread.
. . . As thy days, so shall thy strength be.

Matthew 6:34; Mathew 6:11; Deuteronomy 33:25

Walked down by the little stone wall tonight. The grass was soft and wet to my bare feet. Saw a star fall—just a silver inch of light in the darkness, quickly gone. The memory of its beauty is a lovely parable.

July 7—Daily Light is perfect for this morning; "Yet learned he obedience by the things which he suffered."

Hebrews 5:8

How could the Son of Man need to learn obedience?

Another translation of that last verse speaks of the school of suffering. Christ took the course. He asks us to take it, too—but not alone. He calls us into the comradeship of fellow students, disciples, willing to undergo the rigorous program that the Father prescribes for the Son. It's the same figure of speech used in Deuteronomy for the Israelites: "Take this lesson to heart: that the Lord your God was disciplining you as a father disciplines his son. . . . For the Lord your God is bringing you to a rich land, a land of streams, of springs and underground waters gushing out in hill and valley. . . . . It is a land where you will never live in poverty nor want for anything. . . ."

The only land I could imagine that fitted that description was one where I would be Jim's wife. That would be a rich land. There would be streams, springs, waters gushing out—every kind of thirst quencher. There, surely, even if we lived in a tent or a thatched hut, we would never live in poverty or want for anything.

I had much to learn. Jesus was saying to me what He said to His disciples: "There is still much I could say to you, but the burden would be too great for you now."

25

Nobody Knows
the Trouble

August 13—*"What his own soul has felt as bitter pain
From making others feel should man abstain."*

*And from Amy Carmichael's If: "If I make much of anything
appointed, magnify it secretly to myself or insidiously to others; if
I let them think it 'hard,' if I look back longingly upon what used
to be, and linger among the byways of memory, so that my power
to help is weakened, then I know nothing of Calvary love."*

*Dear Lord, Thou alone knowest the inmost workings of my
mind and heart. Keep the level of my love in Christ—never lower.
Thou hast said, "Neither are my ways your ways." Help me to
walk in Thine, Lord, in peace.*

Few things have the power to make us feel as sorry for
ourselves as has loneliness. We feel marooned, cheated.
Everyone else in the world seems to have somewhere to

go, someone to be with, something to enjoy. We alone have been excluded. We simply want to wallow. For me this temptation was strong. I was still in Oklahoma. There was still no link of any kind with Jim. I found something stronger than the temptation, however, in the words of the Tamil proverb and Amy Carmichael. It helped to develop in my soul tensile strength—resistance to stress, the kind of strength that can bear stretching without tearing apart. If it had been thirty years later, I would have been reading an altogether different kind of advice, I suppose, the sort that encourages us to make others feel our pain as vividly as possible, to "make much of anything appointed." There is weakness and the encouragement of weakness in this tendency. It is one thing to try to feel another's pain. We are to bear one another's burdens and thus fulfill Christ's law. He bore all our griefs, infirmities, and sorrows. But we are told also to bear our own burdens. This must mean to shoulder them bravely, to think twice before laying them onto the shoulders of others who may be more heavily laden than we are. It means what the Tamil proverb means. Above all, it means learning Calvary love—forgetfulness of self in order to be strong to serve.

I was not strong in myself. If I had never known that before—but of course I had—I became acutely conscious of it through loving and missing and desperately needing Jim. It was a kind of weakness that surprised and humiliated me. Why should I need him? "Got along without him before I met him, gonna get along without him now," to paraphrase an old song. I wasn't doing very well without him, and here was another lesson. When there is real weakness, especially of the kind that surprises and humiliates us, it is our opportunity to learn what Paul had to learn through his "thorn": the grace of God is all we need, for ". . . power comes to its full strength in weakness. . . ."

My prayers were something like this:

For my loneliness, Lord—Your strength.
For my temptation to self-pity, Lord—Your strength.
For my uncontrollable longings for this man, Lord—
Your strength.

Jesus knew human loneliness in its most poignant forms. As a boy of twelve He was misunderstood by His earthly parents. His obedience to His Heavenly Father caused them grief. In His public ministry He was usually with crowds who came after Him to see what they could get out of Him or to criticize, cross-examine, attack. With those twelve whom He chose as His intimates, there were arguments, misunderstandings, and in the hour of His greatest need, abandonment. Only in the flesh could Christ enter into our destiny, understand our temptations, and be fully Redeemer and Savior. Who can save us who does not come down into our sufferings and experience our pangs? There was nothing I was experiencing that He had not been through in some form. The love that is everlasting had entered this world, my world, my very heart, known its struggles, shared its weakness and perplexity. None of those things then would separate me from His love. They would, in fact, give me the opportunity to experience it, to learn to cry, "Abba, Father!"

"In that cry the Spirit of God joins with our spirit in testifying that we are God's children; and if children, then heirs. We are God's heirs and Christ's fellow-heirs, if we share his sufferings now in order to share his splendour hereafter."

118

26

A Letter at Last

When our paths, to my immense joy, crossed in September of 1948, Jim told me he felt that God had given the liberty to start a correspondence. We talked again about marriage, puzzling over the thought that for us it might amount to an admission that Christ was not sufficient. This idea came out of Jim's reading of 1 Corinthians 7:37, "But if a man is steadfast in his purpose, being under no compulsion, and has complete control of his own choice; and if he has decided in his own mind to preserve his partner in her virginity, he will do well." Jim had underlined in the hymnal he had given me the hymn, "Have I an object, Lord, below, which would divide my heart with Thee?" If marriage was not to be for us, then Christ was going to have to suffice. If with Himself He was going to give us marriage also, then we would receive it as His gift. The thing about gifts is that they are not asked for, but given, freely and out of love. It seemed too good a thing to hope for, but we hoped.

As the train took me to Bible school in Alberta, Canada, I was reading the Book of Colossians as we crossed the bleak prairie of North Dakota—God's great secret, *Christ in you;* warnings about forced piety, self-mortification, severity to the body. How could I tell if this was what I was guilty of? Often during that school year our principal, L. E. Maxwell, would say, "The hardest thing in the world is—," and he would let the students finish it: "to keep balanced." I was finding that true.

On October 4, 1948, the girl who delivered the mail in the dormitory slipped the first letter from Jim under the door. I opened it with shaking fingers. I was hoping he would begin with "Dearest Bett," but he took refuge in the single ministerial word, "Beloved." The letter was type-written, which made it seem impersonal and also caused me to wonder if he would be filing carbon copies.

It's hard to pull out of the nebulae that has collected in thinking about this letter some clever point with which to impress you right off, so I won't attempt it, but proceed as if I had been writing in my present capacity for a good long time. Got your card Wednesday afternoon. Clever, devas-tatingly so. [The card said only, "Miss you. Bett."]

I wish I had a "feel-o-meter" to transcribe what has been going on inside for the last few days. It began with that word I think I spoke to you of when we were together in the chapel that last morning: *trembling.*

And what should a tuffy like me be trembling about? Three things: you, me, and God. You: I tremble to think that my forwardness in declaring my feeling to you is actu-ally affecting your entire life. I have an idea that it will be almost impossible to discern the Lord's mind for you with-out your struggling through a maze of thought and feel-ing about me. You must know a bit of this already in put-ting in an application to a mission board in Africa. And what if, in a real test, your feeling should overcome your faith? Whose then the responsibility? *Not entirely yours.* For this I fear, that I, stepping out of the path of the Lord for just a moment, should draw you with me and thus be accountable for the "loss" of two lives.

Me: I cannot for the life of me understand my heart. Somewhere down deep in the murky pools of consciousness there is a great monster whom I will name "Want" just for now. This is the only constant thing about me: desire. Much to Freud's consternation I cannot name it "sex urge," for I have found that such will not glut the maw of the brute; he demands more of a varied diet, and one not so easily obtained as that, either. I am very thankful that the Buddhist *Nirvana* is not the apex of the spiritual life, or I should be the least spiritual of all men, if absolute satiation were the ideal. The brute is not the spirit or the soul, least of all is he the body. Rather, he is the ME that talks about these other things, argues about them, laughs and asks for more. He is Life. He is submerged down there a-lusting after something he can't name. The nearest he can get to it is with the word *God.* And God feeds him when I allow it. Silly, isn't it? For who, then, am "I"? Well, I didn't intend that this should run into metaphysics, but what I want to say is that there is within a hunger after God, given of God, filled by God. I can only be happy when I am conscious that He is doing what He wills to do within. What makes me tremble is that I might allow something else (you, for example) to take the place that my God should have. Now something tells me that I can, maybe, have them both. I am not averse to this, understand. I only tremble that I should think wrongly in supposing that you are one of the ways in which God intends to come in.

God: or better, the Lord Jesus. I tremble lest I should in any way offend my Eternal Lover. And whatever passes between us let us take note of this: All shall be revoked at His command. I am such a great, cumbersome boor to be "dove driven." Oh, how delicate are the tuggings of my Beloved, and how calloused my responses. Above all else I will that He might find in me the travail of His soul and be satisfied. But this is a hard thing when I speak to you, for somehow, the pleasing Him and the getting you are in conflict. I don't pretend to explain it; I can only describe what I feel—and that not very adequately.

Since you left it has been as if a film has been over my soul. My genuine fervor in prayer was gone for two days. Too much rubble so that I couldn't get to building the wall. See Nehemiah 4:10 for this. Notice, it was not the outward opposers that hindered the work so much as the inward clutter. Not "destruction" from outside forces so much as "decay" within. But the proof of God's hand comes in the affirmative answer to Sanballat's mocking in verse 2. "Will they revive the stones out of the heaps of rubbish which are burned?" The zealous Jews did. Apply this to us and imagine a little while. Are we willing to build with a trowel in one hand while our other hand grasps the sword? The building (God's work) must go on, and if there is to be battle as we build, very well, let us strengthen the "lower places" (v. 13). And I say to you the words of Nehemiah to the nobles, "The work is great . . . we are separated. . . . God shall fight for us" (vv. 19, 20).

I must confess to you, Bett, that I have had regrets about going even as far as we did in physical contact, and that was very little as most judge. We must guard against this if we are ever together again, for it gave me a whetted appetite for your body that I have found to be "rubble" in getting to the work. You must be hard on me in this; I know we do not have the same mind or makeup, and I feel that I need more of yours than you need of mine. Nietzsche has a word for us here: "One must discontinue being feasted upon when one tasteth best; that is known by all who want to be long loved." Do you get what he means by this: "Far too long hath there been a slave and a tyrant concealed in woman. On that account woman is not capable of friendship: she knoweth only love"? This is what I found in Billy—neither a worshiper (though he loved me) nor an overlord (though he was most esteemed). We met as equal dogs at the feet of the Omnipotent. I would have it this way with you and me. Fear not to hurt me with the Living Sword, yea strike to this purpose. Be more than a lover—be a friend. We spoke of this at the moonrising tryst. "Love one another, as I have loved you." Remember?

But how shall I praise the Lord for removing the film this very morning? Confession is good for the soul; it was imperative for mine this morning. I cast it all upon him and John's truth about "cleansing from all sin" was very precious. Oh, how sweetly He "preached peace" to one that was far off (Ephesians 2:13, 17) . . . Nearness was the theme of my song and the thoughts seem well expressed in #136, Little Flock hymnal. The vail is rent, our souls draw near - / Unto a throne of grace; / The merits of the Lord appear, / They fill the holy place.

Oh, Betts, let us 'undistracted be' in our following.

Just to show you what a poor journalist I am, I will quote my time in composition of this letter: two hours. Part of it due to typing, I'm sure.

Have you been delivered after the fashion of Psalm 116:8, "Thou hast delivered my soul from death, mine eyes from tears, and my feet from falling"?

Tenderly,
Jim

27

Whetted Appetites

That "film over my soul" that Jim wrote about, those "regrets about going even as far as we did in physical contact," that "whetted appetite," that "rubble"—what about all that?

A question of chastity. An outmoded word, the world says, but the truth is it's a Christian obligation. It means abstention from sexual activity. For the Christian there is one rule and one rule only: total abstention from sexual activity outside of marriage and total faithfulness inside marriage. Period. No ifs, ands, or buts. Monks and nuns take vows of chastity, which for them means a lifetime of continence, since they do not marry. Some of them are trying to change that. A group of monks near Boston has recently been exploring "alternatives for sexual expression outside marriage." They chose a good area for it, I'm afraid, but monks of all people need not waste their time. It's all been done. Every alternative is being explored every night in the forty colleges and universities (not to men-

124

tion theological seminaries) in that city. Let monasteries be devoted to other things.

The physical contact Jim referred to was my taking his arm when we walked, our sitting with shoulders tightly pressed together, and on one occasion as we sat on a park bench his suddenly stretching out on his back with his head in my lap. My fingers entwined his hair.

Chaste means "not indulging in unlawful sexual activity." Who would accuse us of having done so?

We were trying to live honestly before God, not before any worldly tribunal. Our Christian contemporaries were necking in cars (*scrunching* was the current word in our college), holding hands on campus, kissing in the dormitory lounges. When speakers came to campus, the question students always asked was where to draw the line, how far could they go?

We recognized that we were strongly drawn toward each other. There were "butterflies" when we were near. Those perfectly human, perfectly natural appetites were being whetted with every slightest touch, and the idea of a good long scrunch or even a single short kiss seemed like heaven itself.

Honesty required us to admit that we could not be sure precisely where the "line" *should* be drawn, and it was a potentially unmanageable force we were dealing with. Chastity meant for us not taking lightly any least act or thought that was not appropriate to the kind of commitment we had to God.

First things first. God's work was what we were seeking first, a "building." "Are we willing to build with a trowel in one hand while our other hand grasps the sword?" Jim asked. Difficult to see how we could be indulging in other distractions at the same time.

All that is perfectly human and perfectly natural in us must first be offered. The body must be a living sacrifice, holy and acceptable to God. It does not become inhuman and unnatural by this offering, any more than the body God prepared for His Son, Jesus, which was offered back by Jesus to the Father, became inhuman and unnatural by His offering. It is still human; it is still natural. But it is holy. And acceptable.

This is the will of God, that you should be holy: you must abstain from fornication; each one of you must learn to gain mastery over his body, to hallow and honour it, not giving way to lust like the pagans who are ignorant of God; and no man must do his brother wrong in this matter, or invade his rights, because, as we told you before with all emphasis, the Lord punishes all such offences. For God called us to holiness, not to impurity. Anyone therefore who flouts these rules is flouting, not man, but God who bestows upon you his Holy Spirit.

28

How Much Can a Kiss Tell You?

"How in the world can you tell if you want to marry somebody if you've never kissed them?" I've heard students say. My reply, "But how in the world can you tell you want to marry somebody just because you've kissed them?"

Intimacy is not necessary.

When Abraham sent his servant to find a wife for Isaac, there was no question of any tryouts by means of intimacy. The servant, the third party, had to look her over and assess her worth and suitability. He went to the logical place—the spring outside the city, where the women would come. He prayed silently, watching all the time. He had specifically asked God to give him a sign: The girl whom he asked for a drink would not only give him one, but would also water his camels. The servant continued "watching quietly to see whether or not the Lord had made his journey successful."

It was Ruth's mother-in-law, Naomi, who made the choice of a husband for her and told her exactly what moves to make. A good portion of the human race has had arranged marriages, and the rate of success of that kind seems to have been far higher than of our do-it-yourself kind. A missionary told me recently of the marriage seminars he is holding for Indians of Northern Ontario. "You mean they have marital problems?" I asked. (The Indians I worked with in South America never thought of marital problems.)

"Do they ever!" he said. "Ever since they began to follow the white man and gave up arranged marriages."

There is not much likelihood that our society will ever consent to arranged marriages. We are stuck with our ill-defined system. Even so, one can learn much about a prospective mate by observation alone.

There is no better place than a college campus to observe what a man or woman is made of. From a respectful distance, with no knowledge on his part, I had the opportunity to observe the character of Jim Elliot. I have told how I watched him in the dining-hall lines, with his little packs of cards—a man who was careful with his time. I watched his friendliness and enthusiasm. I knew what kind of student he was. I watched him wrestle (he won a championship in four states), watched him lead the Foreign Missions Fellowship, heard him pray. There was nothing pompous or stuffy about him. I noticed his clothes. He spent very little on them—wore the same two or three pairs of trousers and the same jacket and sweater for years. He had hardly any notion of styles or colors, but he was not sloppy. Not that this proved he was the man I was looking for, but it gave me a hint that his primary concern was not clothes. When we began to get better acquainted through conversation, I found my hunches verified. Long before I had any reason to think he might be interested in me, I had put him down as the sort of man I hoped to marry. Kissing and holding hands would have added nothing to this conviction (anybody can kiss and hold hands). On the contrary, in fact, it would have subtracted something very important. I wanted to marry a man prepared to swim against the tide.

I took it for granted that there must be a few men left in the world who had that kind of strength. I assumed that those men would also be looking for women of principle. I did not want to be among the marked-down goods on the bargain table, cheap because they'd been pawed over. Crowds collect there. It is only the few who will pay full price. "You get what you pay for."

These were the words of the Lord to me, for his hand was strong upon me; and he warned me not to follow the ways of this people: You shall not say "too hard" of everything that this people calls hard; you shall neither dread nor fear that which they fear. It is the Lord of Hosts whom you must count "hard," he it is whom you must fear and dread.

It is a powerful lie that, because sexual desire is natural, healthy, and God-given, anything I do because of that desire is natural, healthy, and God-given.

"How can anything that feels so good be so bad?"

"Intimacy is an act of worship."

"Denying yourself the expression of that desire is dangerous—it's repression, it'll lead to perversion and so on."

"Nobody can control all that fire when he's young."

Lies, all of them.

Christians who are buying such rubbish today are without honor. They have lost the notions of fidelity, renunciation, and sacrifice, because nothing seems worth all that. There is nothing for which they will pay the price of actual, conscious, painful, down-to-earth self-denial—*except* (and I am convinced this is a significant exception) visible gains like money and sports. If young people have

129

heroes today, they are athletes. If they have role models of endurance and sacrifice and self-discipline, they are athletes. If a man denies himself comforts, vacations, pleasures with his family, evenings at home, or the free indulgence of whatever appetite he feels, it is usually for money. Nobody will worry very much about his being repressive or fanatical or weird, so long as money is his motive.

If your goal is purity of heart, be prepared to be thought very odd.

29

They Abstain
From Nothing

How shall I speak of a few careless kisses as sin to a generation nurtured on the assumption that nearly everybody goes to bed with everybody? Of those who flounder in the sea of permissiveness and self-indulgence, are there any who still search the sky for the beacon of purity? If I did not believe there were, I would not bother to write.

Purity, I fear, has gotten mixed up in people's minds with the caricature of Puritanism, which, in the popular imagination, is a dour, brittle revolt against all the pleasures of the flesh. Puritans were in fact very earthy people, robust in their affirmation of life, not by any means "Victorian" (another word grossly misunderstood today in being made a synonym for all that is negative). Neither the concept of purity nor the doctrines of the Puritans deny life. Rather they refer back to the very Giver of Life Himself. Purity means freedom from contamination, from anything that would spoil the taste or the pleasure, reduce the power, or in any way adulterate what the thing was meant to be. It means cleanness, clearness—no additives, nothing artificial—in other words, "all natural," in the sense in which the Original Designer designed it to be.

Can I say categorically that a kiss is a sin? I can say that it might be. I can say that it might take the edge off, spoil the taste and the pleasure later on. It might reduce power. It might distract the heart. I do not want to be guilty of Pharisaism. Jesus condemned the Pharisees for teaching as doctrines the commandments of men. They professed much; they exemplified little of what they professed. Their worship was in vain, for they paid lip service while their hearts were far from God. It is the heart's direction that is always the central issue. God knows what the heart is set on. We can deceive others. We can easily deceive ourselves. The humble and honest heart will always be shown the truth.

". . . Of course we all 'have knowledge,' as you say. This 'knowledge' breeds conceit; it is love that builds. If anyone fancies that he knows, he knows nothing yet, in the true sense of knowing. But if a man loves, he is acknowledged by God." Paul wrote that to people who were confused about whether it was right or wrong to eat food that has been offered to idols. "Certainly food will not bring us into God's presence: if we do not eat, we are none the worse, and if we eat, we are none the better. But be careful that this liberty of yours does not become a pitfall for the weak. . . . If food be the downfall of my brother, I will never eat meat any more, for I will not be the cause of my brother's downfall."

It was the principle of love that constrained Jim and me to tread so lightly, to hold each other at arm's length, knowing we belonged first to Christ, wanting Him to claim our hearts' affections before all others.

William Wilberforce wrote in *Real Christianity:*

Measure your progress by your experience of the love of God and its exercise before men. . . .

In contrast, servile, base, and mercenary is the notion of Christian practice among the bulk of nominal Christians. They give no more than they dare not withhold. They abstain from nothing but what they dare not practice. When you state to them the doubtful quality of any action, and the consequent obligation to refrain from it, they reply to you in the very spirit of Shylock, "they cannot find it in the bond."

In short, they know Christianity only as a system of restraints. It is robbed of every liberal and generous principle. It is rendered almost unfit for the social relationships of life, and only suited to the gloomy walls of a cloister, in which they would confine it.

But true Christians consider themselves as not satisfying some rigorous creditor, but as discharging a debt of gratitude. Accordingly, theirs is not the stinted return of a constrained obedience, but the large and liberal measure of voluntary service.

That says it well—a debt of gratitude, a liberal measure of voluntary service. I can press those on no one as "law."

A man's love for a woman ought to hold her to the highest. Her love for him ought to do the same. I did not want to turn Jim aside from the call of God, to distract his energies, or in any way to stand between him and a thoroughgoing surrender. This was what I understood real *love* to mean. "And love *means* following the commands of God. This is the command which was given you from the beginning, to be your *rule of life*."

"Well, it's okay for them. It doesn't mean everybody has to. . . ."

God leads His dear children along different pathways. But He asks the same brand of commitment of all of them. *Everybody* who wants to follow Him has to:

give up self,
take up the cross,
follow.

This means trying every day to do what He says to do and not to do what He says not to do.

There are things to be aimed at and things to be shunned. We may not like the "dos and don'ts," but they are in the Bible. Paul had many very practical instructions for the young man Timothy. He told him to have nothing to do with foolish and ignorant speculations, to avoid empty chatter, turn from the wayward impulses of youth and pursue justice, integrity, love, and peace with all who invoke the Lord in singleness of mind. Repeatedly he urges him to keep out of useless argument and to be himself a living demonstration of what he preaches. This is good teaching for us today. Those who prefer argument to obedience we must leave alone. "For the time will come when they will not stand wholesome teaching, but will follow their own fancy and gather a crowd of teachers to tickle their ears. They will stop their ears to the truth. . . . But you yourself must keep calm and sane at all times; face hardship, work to spread the Gospel, and do all the duties of your calling."

30

A "Small" Sin

"He gave me freedom to write if I pleased—for me, there is no sin in it," wrote Jim a few weeks after we had begun our correspondence, when I, as usual, was full of misgivings as to whether we did right.

So long as my conscience remained pure toward God in relation to you, the Spirit freed me to write as I pleased. But, in this, my liberty may have now become license in carrying things too far for you to endure, should our relation be cut off. I am ready now to renounce our correspondence if my liberty has come to its end in imposing itself upon you with harmful results. Now I feel it is your place to precipitate discontinuance. You know best what our writing is doing to you. My answer from the Lord about marriage or engagement is now a decided *no* so long as present circumstances prevail, with no conditions as to what might happen when and if they change. Can you afford to continue to feed a growing love which may be cut off without any fulfillment at some future time? One word from you will settle it.

The word from me was that we would keep on writing. Jim's freedom freed me.

A strange thing happened during Jim's senior year in college. He called it his Renaissance—a new openness to social life, friendships with people he did not consider specially "spiritual," the freedom to date if he felt like dating, and a great deal of clowning, giving vent to his native flair for acting and mimicry. I heard of it secondhand and was offended. What had happened to him?

A psychologist could explain it easily no doubt. Jim's explanation was simply that the Lord had liberated him from some old restraints, enabling him to reach out, break barriers, enjoy things. He admitted that he carried it too far. There were some "kissing incidents" reported to me in letters from other students. I asked him about those, and he answered,

> I stood there, said and did as you have been told, entirely in the flesh. And the same "me" wrote of "purity in love." You may judge which, whether flesh or spirit, prompted me in this latter. For the fact that it has blackened my conscience, hurt you, stumbled others, and brought dishonor to Christ, I now experience overwhelming sorrow. The act, the effect of it, the regret for it shall be consumed by the flashing of my Judge's eye, and I shall suffer loss. There's an end of it, and a costly one.

The notion was not a new one—that the relationship that means most in a man's life is governed by far stricter principles than the casual ones. Because the girls he had kissed did not "mean anything" to him, he took it lightly at first. I didn't. I had expected perfection in Jim or at least the strength of consistency. I did not find it, nor did he, of course, find either perfection or consistency in me, but he repented.

136

I do not know the tearful repentance I should like to for having wandered and caused others to stray as I did. Dr. Brooks [the dean] is right in saying that I have much to regret in seriously looking over the past year. But with that statement I must also say I have tremendous thanksgiving to God at the same moment. Impossible, you say? Very well, but that is how it stands. I have confessed to God, to the senior class, to the Foreign Missions Fellowshipers, to you, to other individuals. And I am eased. If there is more that I must do, I stand ready for reproof. Do you expect yet more of me?

What more could I expect? Jim Elliot was a man. Men are sinners. That was the simple truth. He was my ideal, but I had to come to terms with the truth. He had disappointed me. Hadn't I disappointed him many times?

"If we claim to be sinless, we are self-deceived and strangers to the truth. If we confess our sins, he is just, and may be trusted to forgive our sins and cleanse us from every kind of wrong; but if we say we have committed no sin, we make him out to be a liar, and then his word has no place in us. . . . Jesus Christ. . . . is himself the remedy for the defilement of our sins. . . ."

31

A Cave
and a Driftwood Fire

Jim's next letter began with an original poem.

And dost Thou hear the *silence* of my heart, Lord;
Canst Thou count the tears that never reach my eyes?
And these yearnings, which will not fit my words, Lord;
Wilt Thou feed this hidden hunger—
Desire, spawned of the Spirit, which somehow fails to
    rise?

"Yea, Soul, Eternity has tuned my ear to silence,
My own heart brims with tears now long unshed;
The quiet sanctuary of unspoken reverence
Is my dwelling place of old;
And in the deeps of spirit have I made my bed."

A whole year went by before I saw Jim again. We cor-
responded, but not often. I finished the Bible school course,

and he finished college in June of 1949. I went to work with the Canadian Sunday School Mission, in an out-of-the-way place in Alberta's bush country, called Patience. I had need of Patience. Jim sent me Isaiah 59:9: ". . . We look for light but all is darkness, for the light of dawn, but we walk in deep gloom."

His mother wrote in August to invite me to stop in Portland on my way home from Alberta. The diary is full of misgivings and assurances—it's wrong to go; it's okay to go; God is leading; no, it's my own determination to get a glimpse of Jim. Should I take the money my parents had sent me as a "sign"? What about the letter from Mrs. Elliot? Would Jim be really glad if I went, or would it put pressure on him . . . and on and on. I accepted and took a Greyhound bus.

From Seattle I sat next to a sailor who was as eager to read a book as I was, so there was no chitchat until we were near Portland. He looked at me and said, "I've never seen anybody sit so still. You haven't moved a muscle the whole trip. Scared or something?" I was sick with anticipation. When the bus arrived in the station, there was no one to meet me. I wandered around, my worst fears seeming to materialize. Then there he was, standing at the wrong place, scanning the incoming buses. His back was toward me. I stopped, wondering what to do or say. Something made him turn, and he broke into the old grin. "Hi, Betts."

The first few days were spent attending meetings at the Gospel Hall. It was the annual Labor Day conference, and the Elliot men were very much in view on the platform as speakers, at the back managing things, milling around as hosts. We had little time for talk until it was over, when we went to Mount Tabor Park. We sat on the grass. *Here it comes,* I thought. But again it was Isaiah 59:9. Still looking for light. Still no word as to whether God might have "changed His mind." Why should I have entertained such a foolish hope? Well, because I couldn't help hoping against hope.

I helped Jim's mother with the laundry one morning, and as she was hauling the sheets out of the machine she suddenly said, "I know these Elliot men. They can never make up their minds. If I were you I'd tell Jim it's now or never."

I knew very well what Jim's answer would be: *never.* I would just as soon leave myself room for hoping. I felt annoyed at her advice. She was putting Jim in the same box with the rest of them, his father and two brothers. I was trying hard to believe that he had a better reason than merely being unable to make up his mind. His mother shook my confidence.

We went to Oregon's magnificent coast for a day. We walked down through the thick fir forest to an isolated cove where we explored sea caves and swam in the frigid Pacific. We built a driftwood fire. Sitting close together, watching the sun sink into the gleaming sea, the temptation to express ourselves, to do what we felt like doing, was nearly overwhelming. Because the final choice had been made long before, by the grace of God we were not overwhelmed.

I write this for one reason. To show that it is possible for two young people, full of all the juices that youth is endowed with by the Creator, to resist temptation.

They can't do it unless they have a motive that makes it worthwhile.

They can't do it alone.

"If you feel sure that you are standing firm, beware! You may fall. So far you have faced no trial beyond what man can bear. God keeps faith, and he will not allow you to be tested above your powers, but when the test comes he will at the same time provide a way out, by enabling you to sustain it."

He enabled us.

140

A word of warning here. It is not a good idea to go into caves or to sit by driftwood fires in lonely places if you are not yet sure of your God. Paul advised the young Timothy to "turn from the wayward impulses of youth. . . ." Don't walk straight into them and then blame God if the temptation is too great for you.

32

How Do You Say No?

At a singles conference in the Northwest last month I was handed a blue slip of paper that said, "How do you tell a guy/gal no? How do you keep a safe distance?"

I smiled inside, thinking of how simple the answer is. You can do it in two ways: the English language and body language. You say no, and you move away.

I'm always having to explain to people that when I say there is a simple answer I do not necessarily mean there is an easy answer. It's easy enough to understand—in other words, it's *simple*. But doing it is just plain hard. There is always that fundamental conflict going on: the good I want to do fighting the evil I don't want to do and the desire that seems to be so good in itself verses the deeper desire to love my Master above all others.

You have to ask for help. Help will most certainly be given. When I pray for this, sometimes the words of an old gospel song that we used to sing in family prayers come to my aid:

Ask the Savior to help you, comfort, strengthen, and
  keep you;
He is willing to aid you—He will carry you through.

The song is called "Yield Not to Temptation." It is the
yielding, not the temptation itself, that is sin. We have to
keep asking the Savior to help us, comfort, strengthen,
and keep us. He is not reluctant. He is willing. He will carry
you through, if you want to be carried through. You must
want to.

Does that mean that my motives must be absolutely
pure then? Does it mean I have to have finally resolved
those conflicts mentioned above? If it did, I'd have no testimony to give. It ought to be quite plain in these pages
that the conflict continued to rage. But the wills of two
people had been offered to God. The love of their hearts
had been committed. He helped us. He carried us through.

One of our times alone together was a trip to Mount
Hood. We took the day to drive to Timberline Lodge and
hike for miles up and around the slopes and Alpine meadows. We ate lunch on the grass by a tiny crystal stream,
where we watched a water vole dive and dart through the
water. In the evening we stopped in a dark fir forest, on
the drive down, to eat the only food we had brought along,
a can of baked beans. Jim had not thought to bring a can
opener, or anything to eat with, so he gouged it open with
his penknife, and I managed to slice my finger rather badly
trying to scoop out my share. I still have a scar. A week
later he wrote:

This hour a week ago we were driving home from the
forest camp, very conscious that it was to be our last night
together. Seems ages ago now that we ate those beans from
one can in the dark. I remember sounding very absurd as
we left the place, saying something about your "militant

morality" and hearing you say something about being thankful—then the long drive in silence and tears. . . .

Do you still believe *God* led you here? I do. I say that without reserve or emendation. Further, I love you now by faith. What God is doing I cannot say, but this I know: *He* has led us together. I am trusting Him in you to perfect these obvious lacks [the reference is to criticisms the Elliot family had of me, which Jim exhorted me to correct]. If these things make you angry or sorrowful to tears, turn again to Psalm 138:8:

Jehovah will perfect that which concerneth me.
Thy lovingkindness, O Jehovah, endureth forever.
Forsake not the work of Thine own hands.

"Fret not thyself" was a comfort last Tuesday night. It is tonight as well, for the tears have gone for me. Would that I knew your eyes were dry tonight. This brings me to another point. Dare we ask the Lord, Betts, in light of our frailty, to take us from this "dwelling in silence"? As I stood watching you weep on the bus (forgive me for not obeying your request that I leave—but I couldn't go somehow, knowing you were still to be seen) Teasdale's "What Shall I Give My Love?"* kept sounding deep within. "How can I give her silence . . . lifelong?" Every time we have parted it has been harder. I do not want to part with you on this basis again. So I have prayed, quaveringly, that the Lord would not let us see one another again without giving us some assurance of His ultimate goal in relation to us. This parting into "undefined silence" is terrible. So, though we might want to be together again this fall, I think it would be better if we prayed, "Lord, show us some word of assurance _____," oh, I can't say it. Do you understand?

*I asked the heaven of stars
What I should give my love—
It answered me with silence,
Silence above.

144

I asked the darkened sea
Down where the fishes go—
It answered me with silence,
Silence below.

Oh, I could give him weeping,
Or I could give him a song—
But how can I give silence
My whole life long?

33

Four Bare Legs

What looked to Jim like "militant morality" was partly the knowledge that is deep in a woman that she holds the key to the situation where a man's passions are involved. He will be as much of a gentleman as she requires and, when the chips are down, probably no more, even if he has strict standards of his own. He will measure her reserve, always testing the limits, probing. This is not necessarily because he wants to go as far as possible. It is sometimes from a confused sense of obligation, or even chivalry, to meet her expectations. I'm sure this is true, because men have told me so. Sometimes, bringing a girl home from a date, they say to themselves, *Guess I've got to kiss her good-night. Wish I didn't have to.* It is a relief when the girl lets him know she doesn't want him to. It can be a relief when she says no, even when he wants to kiss her, because he finds mystery in her, and mystery is both surprise and delight.

"Keep your distance," I say to women. Recognize that fundamental anomaly of human nature, that we prize what we cannot easily get. We take for granted, we even come to despise, that which costs us no effort. The bicycle given for Christmas will not be prized like the bicycle bought with the money earned by delivering newspapers for two or three years.

This propensity is not new. The one thing forbidden in the Garden of Eden was the one thing most desired. The fruit trees that were freely provided were taken for granted.

If there is one reason why sex becomes dull and a bore, it is that it is commonplace. It's available anywhere, everywhere, to everybody who is looking for it. Nothing is kept in reserve. No pleasures are saved for the wedding night, let alone for the bride and bridegroom exclusively.

Friends who run a honeymoon resort in the Poconos have told me that they must announce new activities and recreation at every meal. "We don't want them to get bored and leave. You see, they've had it all before the honeymoon."

I'm really quite a sentimental woman. Some of my reserve had nothing to do with militant morality, or even with Christian principle, but with the very real pleasure of saving things up. The ecstasy of Christmastime for me as a child was the knowledge that there were secrets being kept; things going on behind closed doors; boxes wrapped and hidden away, which were not to be touched until the proper time. I have always loved mystery and surprise.

I used to save the very best tidbit on my plate till last. (I might as well confess it—I still do!) We were not allowed to have dessert until we had eaten all our spinach, and in a way I truly did not want to. My husband now occasionally offers me a chocolate just before dinner. I don't want it. Chocolates belong after dinner.

I have never wanted to read the last page of a book until I have read all the preceding pages. There is pleasure in doing things in the proper order.

Certain things properly belong to intimate love which do not properly belong to friendship's love. Certain things belong to marriage that do not belong to courtship. For everything there is a season, and:

> . . . for every activity under heaven its time . . .
> a time to weep and a time to laugh;
> a time for mourning and a time for dancing . . .
> a time to embrace and a time to refrain from
> embracing . . .
> a time for silence and a time for speech.

Have you noticed that one doesn't see such long lines of cars as we used to see on Saturday nights along the beach or the city park? It was a common sight for couples to be kissing or sitting in laps, making the most of pleasures this side of consummation. Nobody seems to feel it's necessary anymore to put up with the discomfort of a car or to stop short of anything. Why not just go to bed? Nobody will mind. A Christian young man told me that when he went to visit his girlfriend for a weekend, he was taken aback when her mother showed him to the girl's room. Her parents assumed he would expect to share it with her.

Let no one imagine that I am recommending the Saturday night parking routine. I deplored it when I was a teenager. I deplore it now. I am recommending virginity. Virginity for both men and women. If virginity is to be preserved, lines must be drawn. Why put yourself in any situation where the lines become smudged and obscure? Why take the risks? Why accept the pressure of tremendous temptation when you can easily avoid it by refusing to be anywhere where compromise is possible?

Psychologist Henry Brant tells of his son's angry retort when his father forbade him to go out alone in a car with a girl.

"What's wrong, Dad? Don't you trust me?"

"In a car—alone at night with a girl? I wouldn't trust *me*. Why should I trust you?"

C. S. Lewis wrote:

When I was a youngster, all the progressive people were saying, "Why all this prudery? Let us treat sex just as we treat all our other impulses." I was simple-minded enough to believe they meant what they said. I have since discovered that they meant exactly the opposite. They meant that sex was to be treated as no other impulse in our nature has ever been treated by civilized people. All the others, we admit, have to be bridled. . . . But every unkindness and breach of faith seems to be condoned provided that the object aimed at is "four bare legs in a bed." It is like having a morality in which stealing fruit is considered wrong—unless you steal nectarines.

34

His Sublime Keeping

Nearly a year after I saw Jim on my way to Canada, we had two days together in Illinois. He was best man in my brother Dave's wedding, and I was a bridesmaid. We had a few hours alone that evening, then another year of separation. In 1951 Jim and his missionary-colleague-to-be, Pete Fleming, came east to speak in churches that were to assume part of their support. Into his crowded schedule we managed to squeeze a picnic in the New Jersey pines, a lunch at Wanamaker's Tea Room in Philadelphia (I remember the pink mayonnaise on my salad), and a day in New York. We met for breakfast at what seemed to us a fancy hotel. The waiter brought tiny cups of scalding hot coffee when he brought the menus. This, we felt, must be the ultimate touch of class. We went to Radio City Music Hall and saw the film *American in Paris* and late that evening stood atop a tall building, leaning on a parapet, looking at the lights of the city, longing, again, for what we could not have. Jim hinted then that he was beginning to believe that God was going to allow us to be together someday. I waited, trembling with hope that the Great Revelation had been given, but it was the same story. No green light.

A page from my journal of that time quotes from T. C. Upham's *Inward Divine Guidance:* "The disposition . . . to leave the dearest objects of our hearts in the sublime keeping of the general and unspecific belief that God is now answering our prayers in His own time and way, and in the best manner, involves a present process of inward crucifixion which is obviously unfavorable to the growth and even the existence of the life of self."

When the meetings were over, my brother Phil and his wife, Margaret, took the three of us—Jim, Pete, and me—to our family vacation home in New Hampshire. It was mid-October, too late for the glorious autumn colors of the rock maples and the sweet gum trees. Winter had closed in for good, and the old house, Gale Cottage, was frigid without central heating. We spent the days hiking the White Mountains—Bald Mountain and Artist's Bluff, through the Flume and then up to lovely little Lonesome Lake on the side of Cannon Mountain. These mountains were tame to Jim and Pete, who only a few weeks before had "done" Rainier, Adams, and St. Helens. But they were hearty in their appreciation of an older, milder beauty.

One very gray day we took the Ammonoosuc Trail up to Lake-of-the-Clouds on Mount Washington and descended by a steep, rocky trail that threaded alongside a rushing mountain stream. Jim stopped to let the others go by and pointed out to me that again and again the water was separated into two streams by an interrupting rock, but came together at last in a deep, calm pool. An allegory for us, he said.

In the evenings we all huddled around the fire, toasting marshmallows, drinking hot chocolate, while Peter read poetry aloud. The others were gallant in going up early to the arctic bedrooms, leaving Jim and me to talk late and watch the embers die.

In a letter written a few weeks afterwards, Jim wrote:

> I wonder if you were conscious of averting your eyes in many of those fireside sessions, when I looked straight into them. One time in particular I remember—you rolled your head clear away to look into the fire when I wanted to face you. Please don't! I love the look of you. I'm glad I love more in you than looks, so that if I went stone blind I would still have love, but your looks are not disconnected from it. Love you for love's sake only? Not exactly. For love's sake, yes, but for dozens of other things, too, not the least of which is every dear remembrance of your face. The grace of your forehead, the clearness of your eyes . . . "but oh, that *carven* mouth with all its deep intensity of longing . . . !"

35

Impatience

Nothing was harder for a woman in love to endure and nothing was stronger proof of the character of the man Jim Elliot than his restraint of power.

Not long ago a young woman was telling me of her engagement to a man who was not sure what he was going to do in life. Their wedding date was set only a few months hence, but he had no idea how he would support her or whether she might perhaps have to support him while he went on to further study for another degree. She spoke of many problems that plagued them and of the man's "feeling the pain" of this kind of uncertainty when some would consider it prerequisite that he come to a decision before he took on a wife. She (rightly) suspected that I, too, was of that opinion. I asked if they had considered postponing the wedding until the decision could be made.

"Oh, no, we're both too impatient!" was her reply.

The custom of "going steady" is another form that impatience takes. The couple are not ready for marriage or even for the public commitment that engagement ought to entail, but neither are they ready to leave each other in God's hands, "in the sublime keeping of the general and unspecific belief that God is answering our prayers in His own time and way." Each clutches at the other, fearful lest he "get away."

Unless a man is prepared to ask a woman to be his wife, what right has he to claim her exclusive attention? Unless she has been asked to marry him, why would a sensible woman promise any man her exclusive attention? If, when the time has come for a commitment, he is not man enough to ask her to marry him, she should give him no reason to presume that she belongs to him.

"But I don't think I can do that. I'm not the strong type."

Hear the words of a woman alone in a foreign land, entrusted with the responsibility of some hundreds of children and dozens of co-workers. The job was too much for her, of course—in her own strength. She did not think of herself as the strong type. She prayed:

> When stormy winds against us break
> Stablish and reinforce our will;
> O hear us for thine own name's sake,
> Hold us in strength and hold us still.
>
> Still as the faithful mountains stand
> Through the long silent years of stress,
> So would we wait at Thy right hand,
> In quietness and steadfastness.
>
> But not of us this strength, O Lord,
> And not of us this constancy;
> Our trust is Thine Eternal Word,
> Thy presence our security.

36

I Have You
Now Unravished

Near the end of October, 1951, Jim came for a last day or
two to my family's house in Moorestown, New Jersey.
Somebody took the first photograph we ever had taken
together. I was wearing an ill-fitting, dark green suit, Jim
a double-breasted blue one. We stood under the apple tree
in the backyard and smiled as though there were no need
at all of that prayer for the reinforcing of our wills or for
quietness and steadfastness.

We drove the twelve miles or so to the railroad station
in Philadelphia, stopping once near the Camden Airport
to pray and cry.

Jim had one more stop to make for meetings. Then,
seated in the dining car en route to Chicago, he wrote:

> Every minute of the weekend was crammed full with
> sightseeing, visiting, studying, and meetings. And all the
> while I have been unable to think for five minutes with-

out being interrupted by thoughts of you. Your face died with consciousness as I went off to sleep and rose as I woke. Images, attitudes, phrases, looks, embraces, hailed me out of the past few weeks and I nearly succumbed to think that it is not to be again for years, perhaps. I am nearer tears this morning than I have been all weekend. Remembrance of what you said about missing me on waking came as dawn broke this morning, and I thought of you with your slender, white, and empty arms there in a warm bed. This may be a phase—the sort of thing Pete wished me a speedy recovery from. I hope in a way that it is, but as yet it intensifies and shows no sign of let-up. There is no need to analyze. I love you, Betty, and feel it keenly this morning.

I'll not forget your clear, wide eyes vanishing at the station on Saturday. The unfeeling lackey who tugged me back on the platform and shouted, "Watch out for the stairs!" and slammed the cover, cut me out of a pleasure— that of seeing your eyes grow smaller and smaller until they disappeared. I had no tears.

From California, a few weeks later:

Woke early again this morning and shared my devotions with dreams of you. It bothers me somewhat that you are on my mind when I ought to be praying, and it's a discipline not to indulge overmuch in remembering. Not that I feel a conflict—I am assured that loving you is part of my life now—important as eating, and God knows, I need it.

> . . . she watched
> Beside my pillow, told me when I woke
> From the fruition of celestial love
> To drink in, like a thirsty traveler,
> The sweetness of her human love once more:—
> Never so sweet as now. They sin who deem
> There can be discord betwixt love and love.
>
> Edward Henry Bickersteth
> "Yesterday"

When he reached home in Portland from California, he wrote:

I thank my God. Life has been made so much the fuller for His giving me you. I was recounting today as we rolled the last three hundred miles up from Klamath Falls how rich, how *full* (I can't find a better word!) He has made life for me. Sealike, but having no ebb, no not at my fingertips! Nature, Body, Soul, Friendship, Family—all full for me, and then, what many have not, the capacity to enjoy. "And He said, 'Lacked ye anything?' they said, 'Nothing.'" Part of me was lacking until this now—oh, I needed you, neither of us knew how sorely! And even now, though I don't *have* you in the fullest sense, still I do, in a sense I will not when we have known each other.

I'm glad that last is still ahead. Glad I'm not jaded by nights in bed with you, as married couples are. They can bear to sit at opposite sides of the car. I'm glad I still can't quite keep my hands off you, still must be warned not to "muss you up." I have you now unravished, and that is just how I need you now. The schoolboy in me still wonders and is awkward—we've not had "experience"—which takes the edge off. We will, I suppose, get used to each other, the feel and smell and look of one another, but I am glad it is not so now. As I never felt before, I feel now that I must keep myself for you. God knows it is a stay to purity, and He knows how many shakings to purity are ahead.

37

Hold God to His Bargain

In January of 1952 Jim was still at home, making last preparations for his sailing to Ecuador in February. I was living in a sleazy fifth-floor walk-up in Brooklyn, New York, trying to learn some Spanish. Things had happened in the previous six months that pointed me away from Africa and the South Seas toward Ecuador. Jim encouraged me, though we knew rumors would fly and I would be accused of chasing him.

He wrote more frequently now, often skirting very close to and occasionally mentioning the subject of love.

I think that the realism of the Old Testament should make us aware of God's approval of human love. So carelessly we read, "Jacob loved Rachel," and so casually it is stated "she conceived and brought forth a son and called his name . . ." that we forget all that is behind the words, all the tremendous feeling and emotion, ache and satisfaction which the very directness of the narrative tends to subdue. But it is there! It has to be. Well, if it is for us, Bett, we have yet cause for greater praise. For now, let us not slack in being thankful. We have our reasons.

On February 2, late at night, Jim telephoned from San Pedro, California. This was the first time we had ever spoken by long-distance telephone. Ordinary folks didn't do much of that in those days. I trembled when I heard his voice, shook when I heard him say he loved me. My voice shook, I'm sure, in answer to his question, "Do you love me?" I had not meant to tell him, but I had to be truthful. "I can hardly help myself," was my answer. He said goodbye. He was sailing next day.

As soon as he hung up he wrote me another letter.

February 2, 1952. Your voice didn't sound just like I wanted it to—not close enough, and I couldn't hear the quiet aside-laughter. But I thank the Lord for the good feeling of hearing it at all. We talked nine minutes! Surprised? I was. I have to laugh at myself—playing unimpressed all day, hardly able to think through the thunder of my own pulse when I actually hear you. This is the stalwart celibate on his way to Ecuador? I suppose you sensed the same, but no one could tell, watching you. Funny pair, we two, being so different in everyone else's eyes, but so like the race in love. Aren't you glad you "can't help yourself"?

Last night in a dream you were more alive than ever—just your face, near and inviting. Oh, how did I resist kissing you before now?

February 7, 1952. I am seated, shirtless, in our green-toned stateroom, having just finished lunch and a cursory promenade about the deck. Generally, I am possessed of a sense of ease, animated at times with sheer joy at the whole situation. Aboard here we are filled with an abundance which touches the edge of profligacy. Enough becomes too much. For lunch I had oxheart, squash, green peas, and cold buttermilk. Last night it was lamb curry and rice, and yesterday noon roast beef. Before that the memory jumbles, but black cod formed a part of it and the jumble on the whole entirely pleasing.

Your "sense of loss" at our not being able to share things these past few months is not new to me. I know it, and often tell Him about it. And such thoughts as "If Thy dear home be fuller, Lord . . ." [from Amy Carmichael] are a consolation. And then the realistic facing of nonaccomplishment comes to me and crushes to silence all telling. For if, really, we have denied ourselves to and from each other for His sake, then should we not expect to see about us the profit of such denial? And this I look vainly for. It comes to this: I am a single man for the kingdom's sake, its more rapid advance, its more potent realization in my own life. But where is that advance and that realization? I am willing that "my house on earth be emptier," but not unless "His house be fuller." And I think it right that we hold God to His own bargain. I err, of course, in making visible results of our separation the final test, and, I trust, rejoice in seeing beyond results which are obvious. But I reason thus that I should be more importunate in prayer, more dogged in devotion, and should not get, as you say, to a "weary acceptance of things as they are."

Besides this, there is the somewhat philosophical realization that actually I have *lost* nothing. We may imagine what it would be like to share a given event and feel loss at having to experience it alone. But let us not forget—that loss is imagined, not real. I imagine peaks of enjoyment when I think of doing things together, but let not the hoping for it dull the doing of it alone. What is, is actual—what might be *simply is not*, and I must not therefore query God as though He robbed me—of things that are not. Further, the things that are belong to us, and they are good, God given, and enriched. Let not our longing slay the appetite of our living. It is true that our youth is fast fleeting, and I know the rush of wants, the perfect fury of desire which such a thought summons. All that it involves—this getting on to thirty—brings a push of hurry and a surge of "possible" regrets over the soul. And, Betty, this is just exactly what we have bargained for. Obedience involves for us, not physical suffering, perhaps, nor social ostracism as it has for some, but this warring with worries and regrets, this bringing into captivity our thoughts. We have planted (in our integrity) the banner of our trust in God. The consequences are His responsibility.

> We would see Jesus—other lights are paling,
> Which for long years we have rejoiced to see;
> The blessings of our pilgrimage are failing:
> We would not mourn them, for we go to Thee.

38

God Granted
and God Denied

Jim arrived in Quito, Ecuador, at the end of February. Two months later I followed. We were four new missionaries, my colleague, Dorothy, and I living with a family named Arias, and Jim and his colleague, Pete Fleming, living just across the street with a Dr. Cevallos and his family. It was the first time since college days, four years ago, that we had been able to see each other daily over a period of time. We made the most of it. Pete and Jim ate the noon meal with us at the Ariases', and Don Raul, our host, put us through our paces on whatever Spanish we had learned. The competition got hot at times as we raced to master the language, all of us eager to get to the jungle, although Dorothy and I did not know to which part of it we might go. Jim and Pete had promised our senior missionary, Dr. Tidmarsh, that they would go to Shandia, a station in the eastern jungle, with Quichua Indians.

In Quito Jim and I did a great deal of walking. We explored every corner of the beautiful colonial city, visited outdoor markets, churches, parks, museums, indigenous craft shops. We hiked through lovely, lush meadows where sheep grazed, climbed down into deep ravines and up high mountains. We rode the buses nearly every afternoon to the post office to pick up the mail. Sometimes we would see how far we could ride on the one-cent fare.

At the end of our four months together (Jim had been in Quito six months) Spanish study was finished. He spoke it well, and it was time to go. In September he wrote from Shell Mera, the Missionary Aviation Fellowship base from which he would fly to the station nearest Shandia:

> Silhouettes of distant birds are sharp against the clouds, going east—and tomorrow, happily, and in the will of God, I will follow. Only too well I know again the inner weakness to return, to go back to you, but I feel that I have set my hand, and to look back now would be dishonor. He knows the inner part, and He knows how much of me I really leave with you. And He knows why I leave and for how long.

The growth of all living green things wonderfully represents the process of receiving and relinquishing, gaining and losing, living and dying. The seed falls into the ground, dies as the new shoot springs up. There must be a splitting and a breaking in order for a bud to form. The bud "lets go" when the flower forms. The calyx lets go of the flower. The petals must curl up and die in order for the fruit to form. The fruit falls, splits, relinquishes the seed. The seed falls into the ground. . . .

There is no ongoing spiritual life without this process of letting go. At the precise point where we refuse, growth stops. If we hold tightly to anything given to us, unwilling to let it go when the time comes to let it go or unwilling to allow it to be used as the Giver means it to be used, we stunt the growth of the soul.

It is easy to make a mistake here. "If God gave it to me," we say, "it's mine. I can do what I want with it." No. The truth is that it is ours to thank Him for and ours to offer back to Him, ours to relinquish, ours to lose, ours to let go of—*if* we want to find our true selves, if we want real Life, if our hearts are set on glory.

Think of the self that God has given as an acorn. It is a marvelous little thing, a perfect shape, perfectly designed for its purpose, perfectly functional. Think of the grand glory of an oak tree. God's intention when He made the acorn was the oak tree. His intention for us is ". . . the measure of the stature of the fulness of Christ." Many deaths must go into our reaching that measure, many letting-goes. When you look at the oak tree, you don't feel that the "loss" of the acorn is a very great loss. The more you perceive God's purpose in your life, the less terrible will the losses seem.

I suppose one of the reasons I have kept journals and diaries is the desire to gather up the fragments that remain, that nothing be lost. I wrote things there that I could not say to people or write in letters to Jim. I urged him to do the same. "I'm afraid I will disappoint you there," he wrote from Shandia, "I'm losing lots. I don't seem able to record all there is—most of it is in my letters, but a great deal is never expressed anywhere. I sit inside myself and wait for you quietly while star bodies crash through the night skies, Indians die, somebody shouts *ganchai!* in a ball game, I sit and listen and watch and go through the motions of entering in, but I don't, because I feel like history stopped just inside a door in Wittig's house in Shell Mera, months ago."

When that letter came, I thought, *No, I can't stand it. I can't be here, on this side of the Andes, doing all these fascinating things without Jim, while he lives over there, doing all those fascinating things without me.* A few weeks after his leaving

Quito I went down to the western jungle to work on an unwritten tribal language. I wanted to share it all, communicate, enter in, do everything together.

The lesson of the seed had not been fully learned. There must be relinquishment. There is no way around it. The seed does not "know" what will happen. It only knows what is happening—the falling, the darkness, the dying. That was how it felt to be separated as we were—as though we had been given no clues as to why this had to be. "The wanting itself is good," Jim wrote, "it is right, even God granted, but now God denied, and He has not let me know all the wisdom of the denial." We were yet far from the depth of spiritual perception Lilias Trotter had when she wrote those profound words quoted earlier: "The first step into the realm of giving is . . . not manward but Godward: an utter yielding of our best. So long as our idea of surrender is limited to the renouncing of unlawful things, we have never grasped its true meaning: *that* is not worthy of the name for 'no polluted thing' can be offered."

We were given grace to see, however, in our saner moments, some of the wisdom of the denial. Jim was able to live in a makeshift house, with makeshift furniture, letting Indians stream through kitchen and bedroom when they felt like it, and he was free to give attention to language learning and evangelism and the building that had to be done for other people, rather than to me and to a house for us to live in and all the rest. I could occupy myself in a job I could not have done if we'd been together. We were being asked to trust, to leave the planning to God. God's ultimate plan was as far beyond our imaginings as the oak tree is from the acorn's imaginings. The acorn does what it was made to do, without pestering its Maker with questions about when and how and why. We who have been given an intelligence and a will and a whole range of wants that can be set against the divine Pattern for Good are asked to *believe* Him. We are given the chance to trust

Him when He says to us, ". . . If any man will let himself be lost for my sake, he will find his true self."

When will we find it? we ask. The answer is, *Trust Me.*

How will we find it? The answer again is, *Trust Me.*

Why must I let myself be lost? we persist. The answer is, *Look at the acorn and trust Me.*

39

Confused Rollings
and Wheels

Within a few weeks of Jim's going east, I went west, down
to work on the language of a small tribe called Colorado
(named for the red dye with which they painted their hair
and bodies). This meant that two ranges of the Andes separated us. Mail had to travel by mule from San Miguel,
where Dorothy and I were, to Santo Domingo, thence by
banana truck to Quito, where it often remained for days
before being sent by air or road to Shell Mera and then to
Pano. From Pano, the nearest station with an airstrip, it
was carried by Indians to Shandia. Sometimes it was six
weeks between my sending a letter and receiving a reply,
and because we always wrote in longhand, we had no
copies. At times I could not remember what Jim was reply-
ing to.

Riding a bus one day in Quito, I was propositioned by
a huge swarthy man who sat beside me. I wrote of it to
Jim, and he wrote back:

Sept. 27, 1952—I found myself tearing into small stumps and cutting them out with one hack, thinking about it on the airstrip a few days ago. And reading it again today, I found the little ball muscles at the jaw bulge and my teeth clench hard as I pictured it. I am afraid there would have been a scene for sure if I had been on hand, Bett—so it was probably better that I wasn't along, although it probably wouldn't have happened had I been. But what devils me is that he evidently rides the bus line frequently, and it may happen any old day again. It would be maddening but for the trust that I have in God for you. Time and again I have committed the very matter to Him, knowing better and fearing more male passions than yourself. And I am thankful that you are all that you are for such cases, that I can trust you, even if the man isn't ugly next time, and that such things find you, though disgusted and a little afraid, firm and resolutely resistant. And I know that He who has so far preserved us for each other will yet do so, Bett, and for the endurance, make the realization so much the sweeter.

October 8—Oh, I don't know how to tell you, Betty, or even if I should, but our months in Quito put me on an entirely different emotional level toward you than I was on before. Does it sound wrong to say that where you have been given rest since parting, I have had only uprisings of stronger want than ever? Where you have had peace, I find myself at perfect war. I mentioned last letter the strong urge to write, write, write, and the something that makes one restrain. I could add the crazy wish of wanting years to pass suddenly; the old rebellion of "why should it have to be so with us?"; the needing of a place to rest. Could it be that we are crossing the same river, but far enough apart to be at different depths, wisely kept so so that we would not sink together? I seem to feel it all much more keenly out here—there comes a sighing even as I write.

October 27—I have been blessed these last two weeks with *many* dreams of you, which, now that I try to collect them, scatter into nothing more than an exhilarating impression. That first waking agony of rolling over on my cot and not finding you there is not to be borne many days in a row. Still and ever the Spirit gives the comfort of the knowledge of the Will as simply and often I speak with Him of all my desire for you, darling, and wonder before Him at the prolonged denial of a desire for so good a thing. And I pray that what He does for me He does for you, and as often.

Early in December Jim wrote:

This will arrive as near your birthday as anything I can get to you. I well know that you will be twenty-six, and that we have always regarded that age as sort of passing the youth mark. But it doesn't frighten me. You are as fresh and virgin in my thoughts now as you were five years ago, many times more so than much younger women I could name, and I love you with the same boyish vigor that has always held me to you. That last point I hope to demonstrate in perhaps six weeks' time.

Exciting news and disappointing news. He was going to "demonstrate." What did that mean? But he was not going to make it to Quito for Christmas. I had been cherishing the hope that he would.

It looked to me as though it really didn't matter very much to him and he wasn't trying very hard. One thing after another seemed to come up to make it less and less likely. *Where there's a will there's a way,* I thought, and said so.

"I will come when I can with a clear conscience before God and will let you know of my plans if it is humanly possible," he answered. He asked me to give him the benefit of the doubt. He trusted my love, he said, to interpret things in his favor.

Love interprets things in favor of the one loved. I had a long way to go to learn that, but the principle is clear enough in Paul's description: "Love is patient . . . never selfish, not quick to take offence. Love keeps no score of wrongs. . . . There is nothing love cannot face; there is no limit to its faith, its hope, and its endurance."

The trouble, of course, is that we must learn to love *people*. People are sinners. Love must be patient when it is tempted (by the delays of other people) to be impatient. Love must not be selfish, even if other people are. Love does not take offence, though people are offensive sometimes. There are wrongs, but love won't keep score. There are things to be faced, but nothing love can't face, things to try love's faith, discourage its hope, and call for its endurance; but it keeps right on trusting, hoping, and enduring. Love never ends.

The memory of those painful weeks when it became clear that we were not going to make it to Quito for Christmas is still very vivid. I can see now that, humanly speaking, Jim might have changed some things to make it possible. He was not doing all that could have been done to bring us together. My doubts, humanly speaking, were well-founded. But from this distance, I can also see that I should have trusted God in him. Jim, though a human being with human limitations, was trying his hardest to walk in obedience to God. He was not pushing for his own way. I should have rested in that knowledge. Sometimes I did, but often I did not. Jim was concerned with Pete, with Dr. Tidmarsh, and with the Indians. His plans to see me were far down the list. That should have been evidence enough for me that his heart was where it belonged and that, even if I felt Jim didn't deserve my absolute trust when it came to our own cherished plans, God certainly did.

"It is impossible to be submissive and religiously patient if ye stay your thoughts down among the confused rollings and wheels of second causes, as O the place! O the time! O if this had been, this had not followed! O the linking of this accident with this time and place! Look up to the master motion and the first wheel," said Samuel Rutherford in *The Loveliness of Christ.*

We are always held in the love of God. We are never wholly at the mercy of other people—they are only "second causes," and no matter how many second or third or fiftieth causes seem to be in control of what happens to us, it is God who is in charge, He who holds the keys, He who casts the lot finally into the lap. Trusting Him, then, requires that I leave some things to be decided by others. I must learn to relinquish the control I might wield over somebody else if the decision properly belongs to him. I must resist my urge to manipulate him, needle and prod and pester until he capitulates. I must trust God in him, trust God to do for both of us better than I know.

40

Love Letters

When I received the next letter, I wondered that I could have doubted whether it mattered to Jim that we be together. He was losing sleep over it.

Some nights it is lying awake, wondering what it will be like to be alone with you again; others are turbid with wild dreams, everything from embraces to arguments; and still others, like yesterday, are fine until about 4:30 A.M. Then come wisps of hopes and plans that mold and shatter in the mind, little conversation frames, settings, and the mad wanting of the alarm to ring, the "sickness of hope deferred," the cry inside of "how long?" I think sometimes that it will be impossible to meet and speak casually with you, saying, "Hello, Bett," in the presence of other people, feeling sure that my voice will crack or I'll do something that will embarrass us both. But I suppose it will be like always, the greeting, the not-too-long glance into your eyes, the handshake, and the small talk about things that really don't matter. Well, if the Lord preserves me in my right mind until then, I shall be grateful, for, quite frankly, I have never been this way before.

Christmas came and went. New Year's, 1953. The weeks of January dragged by until at last, late one night, I heard the galloping of a horse. There was a knock on the door, and a man handed me a telegram. Jim was in Quito, waiting for me to come. Dawn found me traveling as fast as the mud would allow the horse to go, out to Santo Domingo de los Colorados. Another night, and I caught a banana truck before dawn for the ten-hour grinding journey up to Quito. It was as Jim had predicted—the greeting in the presence of others, the not-too-long glance. But that evening we were alone by the fire.

Jim had waited nearly five years for this. He took it slowly that evening, biding his time. We looked at the fire, spoke briefly of our journeys from the jungle, sat in silence. In the fullness of time, he asked me to marry him. Then— the first kiss. A ring on my finger.

His next letter to me, weeks later, when again the Andes stood between us, said:

Will I ever be able to tell you, Betts, what it does to me to have you call me "darling"? And to know that we are wholly and for always committed to one another, given over to one another's power and pleasure, sold out of ourselves, each for the other's good. The absolute goodness and rightness of it is unspeakable. How shall I say what I feel in gratitude to God for the rights and responsibilities of your love? And what shall I say to you? I don't know. Only this, my darling Betts, that I am drawn to you with a fondness I can never exhibit and held to you with a love that is at once all tenderness and all strength which my very body at either peak of gentleness or power does not suffice to declare. I love you. Once that meant "I trust you" and "I appreciate and admire you." Now it means that I am somehow *part* of you, with you, in you.

Heavy rains in the mountains caused an avalanche on the road from Quito to Santo Domingo, and we were without gasoline for our lamps, staple foods, and, most trying of all, mail. A letter came at last.

> It was hot today and I could hardly force myself to pour concrete into two pillar forms. . . . Hard work, and now I'm ready for bed.
> But not nearly so ready as I would be if you were here. Oh, to be able to take *you* there, darling, and do as I have dreamed of doing with those clothes of yours, and really feel the clean flesh of your beautiful long legs against the broadness of my own. Thunder of Deep Heaven! What gasping bliss that would be tonight. But it will wait for us, and be, as you've said, "perfect" when we arrive there. I long to fondle you tonight, Betts, and whisper that I love you, because I am now

fanatically
—your
—Jim.

> March 22—How shall I tell you, darling, after all I've said carelessly about your features, that now I think them all wonderfully framed? I know when it comes time for me to see them all I will remark with Solomon, "Behold, thou art fair, my love." To me it is satisfying already to know that they are promised me, and only wait God's time for unveiling. Do you know how anxious I am?

Jim went on to tell of a conversation with an Ecuadorian friend who had made a girl pregnant. The willingness of the girl fooled him into thinking all would be well. He had then been framed by her parents, arrested, and forced to marry her. "Such are most of the marriages in my country," was the friend's comment.

"What robbery they must feel, if not shame, at the first intercourse after the wedding under such circumstances.

174

May God preserve us for His time. How Juan could esteem a woman like that I don't know. How grateful I am to God that I am not dealing with the type! Praise, praise for *thee,* lover. Thou art all God planned for me, and I exult in His design!"

Jim planned to visit me in San Miguel in May. In late April he wrote:

These next two weeks will be long ones, I fear, as the rains have come and we must be inside most of the day. I cannot spend hour after hour studying phrases like Pete, and I get wild as a stalled stallion waiting in the radio room, studying the forest across the river and facing the gray, empty sky. I will come regardless of what Pete does or whether the teacher likes being left alone. I need you, darling, and need you soon.

I love you strongly tonight, with a sense of power, a huge, surging hope inside me as to the fulfillment of our love. It is not the quiet longing that is usually on me, but the upflung fists and the shouting for possession, and both arms eager to crush you to me. It is the bursting heart and the wild eye of passion, the laugh that makes the stomach tighten. You cannot possibly understand this, and I really don't ask you to—it is just one of the ways I love you and it happens to seize me as I write. Love is not all a resting in me. It is a tenseness and a daring, a call to crush and conquer. . . . Good-night, my brave lover, and may the God who loves you stronger than I stand guard over you through the night.

41

This Is Our God—We Have Waited for Him

Jim came to San Miguel as planned, slept in the schoolroom, visited the Indians with me, preached in a little Sunday service held for Spanish-speaking white people who lived in our clearing.

On the last evening we stood on the balcony of the creaking old thatched-roof house where I lived with Dorothy. We watched the mist rise in the pasture, veiling the shapes of the few cows, the horse, and the dirty white ox that grazed there. Tree frogs quacked and peeped, an occasional hoot or woodwindlike note came from a night bird. Pinpoints of light from tiny oil lamps in the houses nearby winked out one by one. The moon rose behind tier on tier of jungle trees, its light diffused by the mist.

We talked of plans for a house someday in the eastern jungle. When would it be? Jim could not tell me. We had no wedding date set. He was committed to building houses for two other missionary families. This made me feel resentful. Did it always have to be others first? I could not say this aloud—for disciples the answer was obvious.

A few weeks later he wrote, "Evenings, when we go down to the Talac River to bathe, I spend the whole time looking at the hill I want to build on for us, in reverie and wonder. And my prayers are full of you. Marriage is an *hourly* committal now, and I feel the want of it so strongly that I actually expect something 'catastrophic' every time I am separated from Pete for a while, or when Ed comes to the radio."

The next letter said, "I am fervently praying these days that God will make the day soon when we can live out our love in everyday doings. It may not take anything catastrophic after all to bring us together—just a hurdling, one after another, of the things that block me from marriage now. I may tell you quite freely now, that one of those hurdles, namely, housing, is passed. I feel we could get on in anything to start with, and likely will."

In late June I left my Colorado language work in the hands of two English women in San Miguel and moved to Dos Rios, a station about six hours' walk from Shandia, to fulfill the condition of Jim's proposal—that I should learn Quichua before he would marry me. The pilot had planned to land in Shandia on our way to Dos Rios so that I could see Jim and the station, but weather began to close in, and he would not take the risk. "To see you pass over my head was almost too much," Jim wrote. "I'm not bitter, but I am disappointed, and had to look up to God, going down the trail to visit a sick believer after you had gone, and tell Him that I knew He had something better in mind . . . I had banana and pineapple sherbet made for your arrival, and we soon finished it off after you flew over." (Jim and Pete had a small kerosene refrigerator.)

Letters went back and forth between Shandia and Dos Rios by Indian carriers, and in July Jim came by trail to Dos Rios. I looked out of my window when I heard the shout, *"Chimba-chiwapai!"* ("Please take me across the river") and saw him standing on the top of the cliff of the Mishahualli. By the time I reached the bank, the man with the canoe was bringing him across.

It took some fancy footwork to meet alone during that weekend without scandalizing the Quichua Indians. They knew no such thing as courtship, all marriages being arranged by middlemen and the bride and groom not speaking until after the wedding. It would have been quite impossible for them to believe that we could meet and talk alone without sexual shenanigans. One afternoon I took the trail to a sandy beach of the Mishahualli while Jim took a trail upriver and swam half a mile or so with the current to meet me. At night, long after the Indians were asleep (they went to bed with the chickens, figuratively and literally), we went out into the moonlit meadows, screened from the house by tall pasture grass and orange trees, where we could stand, locked in an embrace, and talk. The matter of a wedding date came up at last. Jim asked how I would feel about November, perhaps January, depending on Pete's reaction, my learning Quichua, Jim's having opportunity to make at least one trek to other areas of the Quichua population. A few weeks later the "catastrophe" Jim had half wished for, an unimagined one, happened. The Atun Yacu, the "Big River" on whose high cliffs the Shandia station stood, flooded in August and carried off, in a single night, all of the mission buildings and several hundred meters of the airstrip. This convinced Jim and Pete and Ed McCully (the new co-worker recently arrived from Wisconsin) that God had something else in mind. They made a three-week trek to the southern part of Quichua territory, found a place in need of a school and a missionary, and agreed that Jim and I were the ones to go there.

We were married in Quito on October 8, 1953. The McCullys and Tidmarshes were our witnesses. Others came to see us off at the airport and to throw rice at us.

At the El Panama hotel, overlooking the Pacific coast of Panama, I picked up the phone shortly after we arrived. "Mrs. Elliot?" said a polite voice. I was stunned. Mrs. Elliot! It was only the front desk, inquiring if all was satisfactory in our room. We went down to dinner and as we dawdled over coffee and dessert, savoring the luxurious atmosphere and enjoying the music of a dance band, Jim looked across the candles at me. "I can hardly believe we've got a bed waiting for us!" he said.

The verse given to us for that day was Isaiah 25:9, "Lo, this is our God; we have waited for him."

It was unspeakably worth the wait.

42

Out of Love and Into Charity

A book about passion and purity ought not to end with the wedding day, for as passion does not end then, neither does purity. While purity before marriage, as Jim and I learned, consists in holding ourselves from one another in obedience to God, purity after marriage consists in giving ourselves to and for each other in obedience to God. Passion, whether that of one who is hungry for another not yet given or that of one who, by God's gift, shares the bed of another, must be held by principle. The principle is love—not erotic or sentimental or sexual *feeling*, but love. It is the way of charity. Perhaps the old word is best. The newer has been corrupted by the strange phenomenon of "falling in love."

I know a young man—I'll call him Philpott—who over the past five or six years seems to have made a career of falling in and out of love. He's a very attractive man and seems able to pick and choose from an eager group of attractive and eminently available women. He wrote to me recently to say that he'd done it again. Fallen out of love with a girl we'll call Cheryl. "Darn it all," he said, "here I thought I'd found my dream girl but 'it didn't work out.' Just couldn't maintain the feelings."

Here's my reply.

About this business of falling out of love. Everybody does it, you know. Sometimes before they get married, but always afterwards. Modern folks simply bug out of the marriage then, if they feel no obligation to keep vows— vows made foolishly, they believe.

There is something to be said for making an adult choice and sticking with it. "Being in love," wrote C. S. Lewis in *Mere Christianity*, "is a good thing, but it is not the best thing. There are many things below it, but there are also things above it. You cannot make it the basis of a whole life. It is a noble feeling, but it is still a feeling. Now no feeling can be relied on to last in its full intensity, or even to last at all . . . . In fact, the state of being in love usually does not last . . . . But of course ceasing to be 'in love' need not mean ceasing to love. Love . . . is a deep unity, maintained by the will and deliberately strengthened by habit; reinforced by the grace which both partners ask and receive from God. . . . They can retain this love even when each would easily, if they allowed themselves, be 'in love' with someone else. 'Being in love' first moved them to promise fidelity: this quieter love enables them to keep their promise. It is on this love that the engine of marriage is run: being in love was the explosion that started it."

So, Philpott, one of these days you need to take a cool, clear look at a good Christian woman. Assess her potentials as a good Christian wife. Is she the kind you'd want as a hostess at your table? Is she what you want for a mother for your children? Is she womanly? Godly? Sensible? Modest? Companionable? Do you think she's "worth" your love? Are you worth hers? (If you think you are, you're probably wrong. Each is to esteem the other

181

better than himself.) Is it God's time for you to get married? Then make up your mind and ask God's help to love her as she ought to be loved.

You said, "One never knows which way the Lord will lead," and that's true. He just might be telling you to "be not as the horse, or as the mule, which have no understanding . . ." (Psalm 32:9) and get with it.

Don't get me wrong. I have no idea that Cheryl is The Woman. Don't know a thing about her except that you said she's gorgeous. That isn't enough. But if you're looking for some kind of feeling that will be consistent day in and day out, forget it. The kind of love that sustains a marriage is God given, but it is also a *daily choice*. For the rest of your life. Never forget that.

You have to choose the woman, with all the brains and good sense you've got, plus all the other methods of knowing what God wants of you (you've read my little book, *A Slow and Certain Light*, about guidance, haven't you?) and then make your move. You have my prayers.

What, exactly, is this "quieter love" that Lewis speaks of?

It is not passion, but neither is it in conflict with passion, when passion is held by principle. It contains and restrains passion. When an unmarried man feels passionate, his love for God (and for the object of his passion) restrains him. When a married man feels passionate and finds that his wife does not, his quieter love restrains that passion for her sake—and for God's. It is just as likely that a woman's passions may be aroused when her husband's are not. She waits then, with quiet love. The question of conjugal rights for the Christian always refers to the rights of the other, never of the self.

"The husband must give the wife what is due to her, and the wife equally must give the husband his due. The wife cannot claim her body as her own; it is her husband's. Equally, the husband cannot claim his body as his own; it is his wife's."

What awful confusion results when these demands are read thus: "The husband must demand from his wife what is due to him. The wife must demand from her husband what is due to her. The wife must claim her husband's body. The husband must claim his wife's body." Nothing could be further from the spirit of true charity, which is always self-giving. Charity says "I grant you your rights. I do not insist on mine. I give myself to you; I do not insist that you give yourself to me."

This selflessness is essential if husbands and wives are to fulfill the commands to love and to submit. It won't work any other way. It is the husband's assignment to exercise the authority of the head, as Christ demonstrated when He laid down His own life for us who are His body. This is self-giving charity. It is not the husband's job to demand obedience. Christ is Head of the Church. He loves, woos, calls, sacrifices Himself. He does not impose His will. Those who will not do His will are allowed their choice, a terrible choice that of course entails inevitable consequences.

It is not the wife's job to demand that her husband love her as Christ loved the Church. Her job is to submit in such a way (that is, gladly, voluntarily, wholeheartedly) as to make it easier for him to love her that way. First Peter 3 is the definitive chapter on this subject.

"Quiet love" was expressed in a letter written by a young woman just engaged.

I do not understand much of society's thoughts and formulas on marriage and the partnership therein. It only makes sense to me the way God stated it so clearly in the beginning. He made woman for man, and within that context the idea of fifty-fifty giving that I hear of does not seem to fit. I want the simplicity and purity of the perspective that when I commit myself to a man in marriage I shall give all that I have to him in love, without any claims to

183

what I desire out of him. Being very aware of my human-
ness and my sinfulness, I know that I shall want, that I
shall, at various moments, know selfishness, restlessness,
and dissatisfaction, but my striving shall remain toward
the higher road of what I believe to be obedience.

Another woman, married ten or twelve years, told me
of her experience of what self-giving had come to mean.
Her husband, a doctor, had made several major moves to
different jobs in different cities. Their homes had been sold,
the children repeatedly uprooted from friends and schools.
When Joan found that her husband was about to make
yet another move, she wrote:

> I found myself saying to God and to Gene, "Listen, I can
> no longer trust you to control my life. I think I could work
> out a better plan than this. I cannot take another picture
> off the wall. I cannot hand the keys to one more house
> over to someone else. I refuse to look like an unstable fool."
> That was the bottom line of my struggle. It sounds so pal-
> try, but I considered trading joy for a shadow. I couldn't
> believe how great was the temptation to trade security for
> God's will. In a very revealing conversation with Gene, in
> which he said, "I can no longer battle you on this issue. I
> will write the letter turning down the job," I saw clearly
> the ghost of the future. If I persisted in insisting that my
> will be done, I was taking away God's and Gene's author-
> ity in my life—killing the joy and love that are the dear-
> est things in my life.
>
> I had been asking God to work, from the beginning, and
> He had brought so many wise words my way. I was ready
> to say, "I'm sorry. I give this up. I do want you to make
> the decision, Gene, and I want God's will and of course I
> can do it." Now this was Christ's life, definitely not mine,
> being manifested. I had been reading *The Great Divorce* by
> C. S. Lewis, a perfect book at the time. And a good friend
> had said to Gene and me, "If you, Gene, are willing to stay
> with a lousy job, if it's what God wills, and you, Joan, are

willing to wander the face of the earth like Abraham for the rest of your life, God will clearly show you what He wants you to do."

Your statement about being willing to go out, not being assured about coming back, but leaving the results to God, was what I needed to hear. Galatians 2:20 [NEB] is our favorite verse ["I have been crucified with Christ: the life I now live is not my life, but the life which Christ lives in me; and my present bodily life is lived by faith in the Son of God, who loved me and gave himself up for me"]. The whole subject of exchange is our dearest topic.

That's charity. In down-to-earth, everyday, tangible, visible, practical, willed obedience. A quieter love, but a long-lasting one, indeed, an eternal one. It means kindness and respect. Old-fashioned "milk of human kindness," and simple, courteous, humble respect for the other person, who is made in the image of God.

Try to remember the vision that "being in love" gave you of what that person was. You found no fault in him or her. "Behold, thou art fair, my love, there is no spot in thee," Solomon said to his beloved. Is it blindness to see a sinful man or woman thus? I think it is a special gift of vision, the power to see for a little while what God meant when He made that person. You find, after marriage, that the person is in fact a sinner, has flaws you never suspected. Try to remember then what the vision showed you. Thank God for it, and treat him or her with the sort of respect due one who will some day manifest most gloriously the image of God.

Charity is the love of God. There is no other way to control passion. There is no other route to purity. There is no other route, finally, to joy.

"Dwell in my love," Jesus told His disciples in one of His last discourses. He put it very plainly: "If you heed my commands, you will dwell in my love, as I have heeded my Father's commands and dwell in his love."

43

A New Act of Creation

"I've already blown it," some readers will be saying. "The standard is impossible. No way can I start picking up the pieces now."

Do our transgressions disqualify us for the Christian life? Quite the contrary. Jesus came into the world specifically for us who blew it, not for those who "need no repentance." ". . . He was wounded for our transgressions. . . ."

If sexuality is a paradigm of the Heavenly Bridegroom and His pure and spotless Bride, how shall we who are impure and badly spotted start over again? ". . . Make no mistake: no fornicator or idolater, none who are guilty either of adultery or of homosexual perversion, no thieves or grabbers or drunkards or slanderers or swindlers, will possess the kingdom of God," Paul wrote to the Corinthian Christians. Sounds as though there isn't much chance for any of us. But then he says, "Such were some of you, but you have been through the purifying waters; you have been dedicated to God and justified through the name of the Lord Jesus and the Spirit of our God." He goes on in his next letter to say, "For the love of Christ leaves us no choice, when once we have reached the conclusion that one man died for all and therefore all mankind has died. His purpose in dying for all was that men, while still in life, should cease to live for themselves, and should live for him who for their sake died and was raised to life."

This teaches us that there is a point of departure. What we were, and what we are in Christ, are sharply distinct. Stop living for yourself, start living for Christ. Now.

"With us therefore worldly standards have ceased to count in our estimate of any man; even if once they counted in our understanding of Christ, they do so now no longer. When anyone is united to Christ, there is a new act of creation; the old order has gone, and a new order has already begun."

My friend Calvin Thielman, pastor in Montreat, North Carolina, tells the story of an old Scottish preacher who, as he was serving the bread and wine of the Lord's Supper, noticed a young girl sobbing at the communion rail. As he passed her the bread, visible sign of the body of the Lord Jesus ("I give it for the life of the world," He said) the girl turned away her face, which was wet with tears.

"Tak' it, lassie," said the old man. "It's for sinners."

For a sample copy of
Elisabeth Elliot newsletter, please write to:
Box 7711
Ann Arbor, MI 48107

Source Notes

Chapter 2

See Song of Solomon 8:4. (24)
Philippians 1:21. (24)
1 Corinthians 6:19, 20 PHILLIPS. (26)
Isaiah 43:1 NEB. (26)
Isaiah 43:2, 3 NEB. (26)
1 Peter 1:18, 19 NEB. (26)

Chapter 3

Robert Service, *The Complete Poems of Robert Service* (New York: Dodd, Mead and Company, 1940), pp. 30, 31. (31)
Matthew 5:8. (31)
W. G. Smith, "A Clean Heart," from *The Keswick Hymn-Book* (London: Marshall, Morgan & Scott, Ltd.). (31)

Chapter 4

Frances Ridley Havergal, "Take My Life." (34)

Chapter 5

Genesis 22:1–3 NEB. (38)
Matthew 19:16, 21 NEB. (38)
Matthew 10:37, 39 NEB. (39)
Philippians 3:8 NEB. (39)

Lilias Trotter, *Parables of the Cross* (London: Marshall Brothers, n.d.). (39)
Romans 8:32 NEB. (40)

Chapter 7

2 Samuel 24:24 NEB. (46)

Chapter 8

Proverbs 14:12, 13 NEB. (49)
Psalm 32:8–11 NEB. (50)

Chapter 10

Anonymous. (55)
Isaiah 40:12, 21, 22, 26 NEB. (56)
Isaiah 40:27–31 NEB. (57)

Chapter 11

Matthew 19:12 NEB. (59)
Isaiah 54:5 NEB. (59)
1 Corinthians 7:34, 35 NEB. (59)

Chapter 12

Psalm 62:1, 2, 8 NEB. (62)
Alfred, Lord Tennyson, *Idylls of the King* (New York: Macmillan and Company, 1939), pp. 755, 756. (62)
Luke 21:37. (62)
Proverbs 17:28 NEB. (63)

Proverbs 19:7 NEB. (63)
Proverbs 10:19 NEB. (63)
S. D. Gordon, *Quiet Talks on Prayer* (Grand Rapids: Baker Book House, 1980), p. 155. (64)

Chapter 13

Numbers 31:23; Deuteronomy 13:3; Psalm 66:10, 12; Isaiah 43:2. (65)
Oswald Chambers, *My Utmost for His Highest.* (66)
2 Samuel 23. (66)

Chapter 14

Christina Rossetti, "A Sonnet of Sonnets, #6." (70)

Chapter 15

Psalm 78:8 NEB. (72)
2 Corinthians 4:11 NEB. (73)

Chapter 16

Amy Carmichael, *Toward Jerusalem* (Fort Washington, Pennsylvania: Christian Literature Crusade, Inc., 1961), p. 95. (75)

Chapter 17

Elisabeth Elliot, *Loneliness* (Gloucester, Massachusetts: Open Church Foundation). (79)
Romans 5:3 PHILLIPS. (81)
Romans 5:4 PHILLIPS (81)

Chapter 18

Edith Colgate Salabury, *Susy and Mark Twain* (New York: Harper and Row, 1965), pp. 249, 250. (83)
Romans 8:35–39 PHILLIPS. (84)
Luke 16:10, 11 NEB. (87)

Chapter 19

Psalm 37:5 (89)
Romans 8:26, 27 NEB. (90)

Chapter 20

1 Corinthians 7:1. (92)
1 Corinthians 7:1, 2 NEB. (93)
Thomas à Kempis, *Imitation of Christ.* (93)
Romans 8:13 NEB, italics added. (95)
Romans 8:7–12 NEB. (95)

Chapter 22

1 Peter 3:4 NEB. (107)

Chapter 23

Stephen Goldberg, *The Inevitability of Patriarchy* (New York: William Morrow and Company, 1974), p. 55. (109)
2 Corinthians 1:12 NEB. (110)

Chapter 24

Samuel Rutherford. (112)
Matthew 11:12. (112)
Deuteronomy 8:2, 3 NEB. (113)
Deuteronomy 8:3 NEB. (113)
Deuteronomy 8:5, 7, 9 NEB. (114)
John 16:12 NEB. (115)

Chapter 25

Tamil proverb. (116)
2 Corinthians 12:9 NEB. (117)
Romans 8:16, 17 NEB. (118)

Chapter 27

1 Thessalonians 4:3–8 NEB. (126)

Chapter 28

Isaiah 8:11–13 NEB. (129)

Chapter 29

1 Corinthians 8:1–3, 8, 9, 13 NEB. (132)
William Wilberforce, *Real Christianity* (Portland, Oregon: Multnomah Press, 1982), p. 123. (133)

2 John 6 NEB, italics added. (133)
2 Timothy 2:22. (134)
2 Timothy 4:3–5 NEB. (134)

Chapter 30

1 John 1:8–10; 2:1, 2 NEB. (137)

Chapter 31

1 Corinthians 10:12, 13 NEB. (140)
2 Timothy 2:22 NEB. (141)

Chapter 32

Horatio R. Palmer, "Yield Not to Temptation," from *Songs for Christian Worship* (Board of Education of the United Presbyterian Church of North America). (143)

Sara Teasdale, "Night Song at Amalfi," from *Love Songs* (New York: Macmillan and Company, 1917). (144)

Chapter 33

Ecclesiastes 3:1, 4, 5, 7, NEB. (148)

C. S. Lewis, "We Have No Right to Happiness," *The Saturday Evening Post,* December 21–28, 1963. (149)

Chapter 35

Amy Carmichael, *Though the Mountains Shake* (New York: Loizeaux Brothers, 1946). (154)

Chapter 37

Anna B. Warner, "We Would See Jesus," from *Victorious Life Hymns* (Philadelphia: The Sunday School Times Company, 1919). (161)

Chapter 38

Ephesians 4:13. (164)
Matthew 16:25 NEB. (166)

Chapter 39

1 Corinthians 13:4, 5, 7 NEB. (170)

Samuel Rutherford, *The Loveliness of Christ* (London: Samuel Bagster and Sons Ltd., 1958), p. 33. (170)

Chapter 42

1 Corinthians 7:3, 4 NEB. (182)
John 15:9, 10 NEB. (185)

Chapter 43

Isaiah 53:5. (186)
1 Corinthians 6:9–11 NEB. (186)
2 Corinthians 5:14, 15. (187)
2 Corinthians 5:16, 17 NEB, footnote for v. 17. (187)

Elisabeth Elliot is a popular seminar speaker, radio teacher, and best-selling author. Her books include *A Chance to Die, On Asking God Why, The Journals of Jim Elliot, The Mark of a Man,* and *Discipline: The Glad Surrender.* For more information on Elisabeth Elliot and her books, please visit her website at www.elisabethelliot.org.